I0624127

SPARKING UP LEADERSHIP

IGNITING YOUR INFLUENCE WITH SPARKLE AND SHINE

ALICIA HUGHES

Copyright © 2024 by Alicia Hughes

All rights reserved.

No part of this book may be reproduced in any form or by any electronic or mechanical means, including information storage and retrieval systems, without written permission from the author, except for the use of brief quotations in a book review.

"I want to tell you a secret that will see you through all the trials that life can offer: Have courage and be kind." – Cinderella

Most times, the simplest things are the things that have the biggest impact. That, and having a sparkly presence and a fairy godmother on your side.

IGNITING THE PATH

A GUIDE TO YOUR JOURNEY

Let's Get the Spark Sparked!

LET'S GET THE SPARK SPARKED!

BOOK APPLICATIONS

THERE ARE copious amounts of books on leadership best practices. Don't believe me? Well, I just googled "books on leadership" and this is what came up:

About 1,460,000,000 results

Seems like everyone who has ever led wants to let you know their thoughts :) And I am, apparently, no different.

What makes my take different? What has my fourteen years of experience as a leader taught me that makes my style unique? Common sense--which isn't all that common! -- combined with a little something extra to make it inspiring, exciting, and energizing for the teams I lead. Because boring does not incite a flame. And dull never gets a big spark. But sparkle and flair drive change and create passion. That's the big bang that will move your team to greatness.

Who Should Use this Book?

- Anyone who is in a funk and feels their greatness is lost in the shadows.
- Leaders who need to excite those in which they serve.
- Those that want assistance exerting influence with smarts and pizzazz.
- Thoughtful humans ready to take a step up into the leadership world and want to ensure they do it with style and grace (Thanks, Big Poppa!)
- Those in charge of remote spaces who need help injecting spark into their virtual landscapes.
- Anyone and everyone who wants to lead and needs a way to do it with positivity and energy.
- Any and every leader who needs a refresh or recharge during a moment of doubt.

ALICIA THE SPARK

FROM AS FAR BACK AS I can remember, I have loved two things: leading and performing. I was heavily involved in dance, school plays, and instrumental performances. Being on stage brought me great joy from the time I was four years old. I was also the teacher's pet. Always chosen to help lead others in all things…. lines, cleanup, projects, etc. I had big dreams of one day being on Broadway with a first runner up career of dancing at Walt Disney World. But as often happens with age, reality started to set in. I realized the chances of either of those were slim. And thus, I began to focus on the more conventional and possible path of education.

The world of education allowed me to utilize both of my skill sets to the utmost. Every single moment of my day was spent on the classroom stage with all eyes on me, putting on a show to inspire those within my charge to love the Constitution, be inspired by Martin Luther King's Dream, and find passion around ancient art and cultures. I was also asked to step into leadership roles beyond my classroom walls…. leading the Social Studies Department, serving on the Principal's Advisory Board, running the school newspaper. And for a long time, this fulfilled me.

Until….

I decided that the thing that was calling me even more strongly than performing was the call to be a mother. And so, after eight years in the classroom, I decided I needed to stay home with my newborn son instead of returning to the school building. I "retired" under the premise that whenever my husband and I were done having babies and that last baby started Kindergarten, I would return to the world of education.

But life has a funny way of not going according to plan. So, when the real estate market collapsed, and my realtor husband was basically out of work for two years, and our savings were long gone, we decided I needed to return to the classroom. I was DEVASTATED at the thought of leaving my two-year-old son and six-month-old daughter in the care of anyone besides myself. When lamenting to a college friend about this great sadness, she suggested I look to teach virtually. And my mind was blown.

Because this was 2009. Virtual education for secondary school students was literally in its infancy in the state of South Carolina. It was an unknown to most (even educators like me) and something that was not really considered a comparable option to the traditional school model. However, I was not only desperate for a job, but desperate for a way to stay with my babies. Therefore, I immediately searched for virtual teaching job opportunities, and lo and behold, a high school Social Studies position was posted at South Carolina Connections Academy. I don't think I have ever applied for anything faster than I did for that position.

I will tell you the complete and honest truth. I did absolutely no research about the school. I assumed I would be sitting at home grading papers and answering emails and was hopeful that I would make about half of what I would make if I returned to the classroom. It truly was desperate times around the Hughes Household.

And then I interviewed in person. With REAL educators asking me REAL questions such as "How are you going to make Social Studies engaging in the virtual space?". And "How are you going to build relationships with students you never see?". I felt like I had failed. My only virtual experiences at that time were through Facebook and email. So, when the Assistant Principal called to offer me a job with an appropriate salary and benefits, I thought I had won the lottery. I get to be at home with the babies AND make full teacher pay?! What a dream!

But y'all, the dream went way beyond that. Way beyond my wildest dreams. Beyond anything I thought possible in education. You see, I went into this role thinking it was a great way to make money while being with my children. And I quickly realized that while that is oh so fabulous, there is so much more to it than that. Because you can actually teach! I mean, really and truly focus on learning and not on all the noise that often takes educators away from that purpose. And you can truly build relationships with the students and staff. Because you have one on one, distraction free conversations with each and can truly listen and learn the needs of the individual rather than half paying attention because of what is happening all around you. And so, what I thought would be a band aid to fix our financial woes became a love and a passion.

And when you love something and you believe in something and you drink that Kool Aid, oh and you have a strong and loud voice, well, you somehow find your way into leadership. People start to ask you to do things. And you WANT to do things to make that place you love and believe in the best possible.

I went from a High School Social Studies teacher to a Teacher Manager, to a High School Assistant Principal to a High School Principal to Executive Director. And although the roles changed, my complete and total belief in staff first and building relationships with all did not waver one second. Heck, it actually grew stronger. AND I got to fully utilize those skills identified as my superpowers from long ago....... performance and leadership. I was able to craft both into a dream profession and back them with time proven beliefs: People first wins every time. Treating everyone the way you want to be treated repays you as a leader tenfold. Common sense decision-making over blindly following all the policies and procedures has never let me down. Great risks equal great rewards.

I am a pretty simple girl. A glittery and sparkly kind of simple. But simple in my thoughts. I trust my gut. I am transparent to a fault (ask my husband) and excitable to a level that is super annoying. I tend to want to jump but have begrudgingly learned that sometimes you do actually have to see what is below before you dive in. Oh, and it isn't always a race to be the first to get it done. Sometimes it is best to let things happen slowly and gradually as opposed to being all in all the time.

Through my leadership roles, my sparky-ness came out loud and proud! I literally could light up a room with not only my excitement and passion BUT with props. I could dress up an email with colors, fonts and emojis to drum up buy in and a following. I could use my blessing and curse of jumping into all the things to my advantage by being brave and taking risks and making sweeping changes. I was able to significantly affect the trajectory of my school, all because of my energy. My magnetic, inspiring spark.

WHAT MAKES A SPARK?

SPARKS ARE LOUD! And always present! Fast and furious! Full of energy and passion and conviction. Sparks like everything colorful and shiny and bright. Boring is our enemy. Commonplace makes us sigh. We are outside of the box thinkers who thrive on risk and innovation. People are generally drawn to us and thus we can inspire many with our sparkle and sizzle. Our energy is boundless (and exhausting), and we constantly must calm our passions internally so as not to dominate conversations or cause distractions and disruptions to the process.

Sparks avoid the tedious work. Which can oftentimes be the most necessary work. Details are difficult for us, as we just want to get to the grand finale. And spelling out every process, procedure and action item can make our skin crawl. We do love a plan, but we certainly don't want to be the one in charge of writing down all those pesky details. We want people to just know how to get there on their own without having to tell them. Because, quite honestly, we don't necessarily know how we are getting there either. We just know and believe we will and are trusting that we can and will tackle anything that comes our way.

As I am sure you know, it is important in leadership to play to your strengths. You must use your superpowers to the fullest and work to curb your deficiencies as much as possible. And, because Sparks live in the extremes, this might be the hardest for your kind. Because Sparks are usually one extreme or the other in all things. There is not a lot of middle ground. Nor uncertainties. Pulling those weaknesses up and modifying them is a constant challenge.

But this is where the sparkiness comes in handy. Because your shine and your sparkle and your ability to influence people will allow you to place a spotlight on those that do excel in your weak areas to do that work and do it well. And you, my spark friend, naturally use that power in all that you do. Getting people to buy into and follow your vision is generally easy for you, because you exude positivity and conviction. You make people believe it is going to work and you are going to succeed. And when everyone is on board, they want to know where they fit in and how they can help.

To truly excel in this leadership space, you must find your tribe and love them hard (I dedicate a whole chapter to this!). Give them things that you know are not in your wheelhouse. And then use your spark power to praise and reward and cheer on those in these roles. Keep your eye on that BIG picture and move it along. Take the risks when others won't BUT listen to those that do like to color within the lines and anticipate all that might come.

And that is how Sparks find their way to greatness!

WHAT IS A LEADER? AND WHAT IS THE MOST IMPORTANT THING THEY NEED TO KNOW?

IF LEADERSHIP only meant telling people what to do, it would be super easy for anyone to lead. Think about it...if there is a task with set steps and it is your job to get the steps done and everyone buys into the tasks, understands what needs to happen, and then gives it their all until the job is done, well, then your job is so easy.

But please consider all the steps leading up to the end.... buy in, clear communication, support structures, answering questions along the way, checking for quality throughout, making sure there isn't a breakdown before arriving at the finish line. Oh, and well, reacting when life doesn't go according to plan and throws everything out of whack. In that context, leading is super hard.

Sadly, people often get into leadership believing if they are in charge, things will be great. And they mostly think about how things will be great for them. Not for the organization and not for the people within that organization, but rather for their own personal gain. If they controlled things, they wouldn't have to answer to anyone. They will get to tell everyone else what to do. They will control the narrative.

But those leaders don't often find great success. They may find temporary moments of grandeur, and if they are in the right place at the right time, singular successes. But their organization's productivity typically will falter, and their potential for overall sustained success will definitely be lacking.

Because "my way or no way," and "do as I say not as I do," and "I run it all" do not allow for growth. For new ideas. For outside of the box thinking. And all those things are necessary for continuous organizational success.

Think about your leadership style.... Are you open to change? Do you allow for constant feedback? Do you seek to look for ways to improve, no matter the cost? Are you willing to think of other processes and allow for differences of opinions? THESE are what make true leaders, not just setting mandates and ensuring they are met.

You know the saddest part of this reflection for me? It is the fact that I can think of all the non-examples of excellent leaders from my past very quickly. Those that did none of the above. I can clearly remember my very first "boss" leaving the teenage me in charge of the ice cream parlor while he went to the bar to get drunk. Literally NO leadership. And I can recall server me being told I had to do all the gross restaurant cleanup work while the "boss" just watched and belittled my efforts the entire time. And I can think of brand new to teaching me with a "boss" that locked herself in her office whenever fights broke out because "that was not her job,". Two things came out of all these interactions.... First was a complete lack of interest in spending any more time than necessary at these institutions, and second, an immediate search began for new employment.

Thankfully, I found the perfect employment eventually. One where PEOPLE were valued, and leaders consistently sought input on decisions. One where staff were given the autonomy to do their jobs in the ways that best suit their needs. One where you trusted everyone to work at their best and highest levels. And not only did the organization flourish, but I did as well! It made me want to come to work each day and contribute at my utmost. It allowed me to take risks and ownership and soar. Which in turn led to continued growth for everyone involved. And the leaders were also allowed to grow and thrive......I am not sure WHY other leaders in other places don't embrace this style, but it is definitely an anomaly. And I guess if it weren't, there would be no need for books such as these!

Be sure to remember to value your biggest commodity, your people. Treat others as you would like to be treated. And, most importantly, remember you don't know it all nor need to dictate it all. This will help you find the greatest success of your career; I promise.

THE SPARKLING CHAPTERS

HOW TO LIGHT UP YOUR TEAMS AND INSPIRE SHINE

SPARKING A STRONG CULTURE
AND KEEP IT BURNING.

A STORY of the power of culture.

I have had a LOT of crazy and big and spontaneous ideas. Like, A. Lot. And sometimes they are GREAT, impact changing ideas. And sometimes, they will crash and burn to the ground, and I am lucky that the whole place didn't go up in flames. But here is the thing......the organization in which I worked was a BIG supporter of creative freedom. Of risk taking. Of trial and error. There was an openness to listen to ALL the feedback and allow for the opportunity to take ideas from those conversations and put them into practice.

As big, crazy ideas came to my head, those above me listened and said go for it! Do it. Take the risk. And when I did those things, those below me said "This is great! We love this! Let's give it a try!". Because they had the opportunity to forge their own path. To take risks. To make mistakes. They would almost blindly follow me, knowing that I valued their creativity, so they wanted to value mine.

One of my biggest whims, which led to my biggest win, came when I decided my staff of about 80 needed to call 1100 customers within 5 days, for us to reach a really big goal that could literally make or break the organization. And I didn't say "stop everything and call,", I said "find time to do this while also doing all the rest." And you know what. They. Did. And not in five days. But in **four**. Because……they knew I had valued them. Over and over and over. They knew I had listened to them and would continue to listen to them. And when they knew that trust was there, and they knew I would do for them what I was asking them to do for me. Well, then it was a no brainer.

And the best part of this story. I truly believe that crazy idea led to us crushing that crucial goal. And that in turn made our culture that much stronger. We had worked together as a team to achieve what seemed impossible. And then we celebrated. And celebrated big. Because we also valued celebration at this organization. And so, the culture chapter came full circle with a risky idea that leads to great celebration.

If you ask a Spark if culture is important, there will be an overwhelming and over the top and enthusiastic YES YES YES. But if you ask a Spark to define culture………wellllllll details just aren't our thing.

But that is the thing about culture. It **is** hard to define. There isn't a culture play book. There isn't a set of guidelines that we can share now and implement later. Culture is something you feel. Culture is something you know is there or is not. Culture is something you recognize is important but are not sure how to describe. Culture is like breathing-it is a necessary and constant part of what we do but not something you even realize is happening All. The. time.

First and foremost, how are you going to make sure this thing that is happening is happening to the benefit of your organization? How are you going to make sure your organization is operating at a high level, with people that not only enjoy their work but are proud of where they work? How are you going to get those that might be on the fence about the things to get off the fence and buy in? How are you going to ensure what you and your organization most value and live and breathe are the things all the rest value and live and breathe?

Well, here is the simplest of concepts…. ask! Have conversations! Find the time to connect and get to know the wants and the needs and the thoughts and the feels of those around you. Use that knowledge to determine the wants and the needs and the thoughts and the feels of the organization. And then marry the two. The needs of the people need to be the needs of the organization. One cannot successfully exist without the other.

Then, begin intentional conversations around those items. In small groups. At your whole staff meeting. Here, there, and everywhere. Make those needs and feels a part of the everyday. Find out the motivators. The most important. The things we just cannot do without.

If food is important to your people, make sure you have it whenever you meet. If time to process is important, be sure to work that into the normal decision-making process. Even if you personally don't care about social time to start or end the day but your staff does, make it a part of the experience.

Find the time to focus on the culture. You just must. You absolutely must. Because even though you can't define it or put it on a Google Doc, you need to give it a space. If your culture thrives on praise and recognition, you better have a standing time in which to do those things. And you better have processes in place that support that need. If collaboration is key to your goals, be sure that you have given space for that collaboration. Culture cannot be an afterthought. It really should be the main thought.

And don't fix it and forget it. Like every great relationship, it takes work. Work on the culture. Check on the culture. Think of ways to improve the culture. What can you do better? What can you take away? Culture is constantly growing and evolving, and without TLC it can wither and die. What worked five years ago will probably not continue to work today. Treat it like you treat anything precious and fragile…. with care and attention. Doing so is the only way to guarantee organizational success.

Virtual Spark Applications:

- Start with the basics. Mandatory meetings. Webcams on. Norms that encourage participation and collaboration
- Create time for culture. Make team building and idea sharing a part of every process and procedure. Every meeting. Every interaction
- Gauge input. Ask what can be done better in the virtual space and then do it if possible.
- Schedule time to meet with everyone. Get to know people on an individual basis. Seek them out intentionally, as you will not have the opportunity to talk to them on the way into the building or at the water cooler-as you would in a face-to-face setting.

HOW TO MAKE FRIENDS AND
INFLUENCE OUTCOMES

HERE'S THE THING. Influencing is all about getting people to feel valued. It is all about THEM even when it is you trying to get them to be all about you! A reverse mind trick. An exercise in the psychological.

Let's keep it really simple for a moment. Let's say you and your significant other are heading out to get a bite to eat, and you really, really, really, really, really want some pasta. Like of all the things you have ever wanted in your life, you want pasta the most. You don't know whatever you will do if you do not get a meal of pasta. But your significant other wants seafood. They need the fried shrimp and the hushpuppies and the tartar sauce or their entire year will be ruined. What is someone to do?? How do you get someone whose mind is so clearly made up and in direct opposition to your desires to switch sides?

There are many tactics you can take. Many approaches to the situation. Many ways you can choose to go.

You can try reasoning:

"I love pasta more than you love seafood".

You can try arguing:

"We ate what you wanted last time."

You can try threats:

"If you don't eat pasta, I will leave you".

You can try anger:

"I hate seafood, and if you make me eat it I will never be happy ever again."

So many terrible choices in which one can try to impact change. And the ones we tend to rely on the most!

But there is a much better way. A way to get someone to side with you on the emotional level. One in which you take out the arguing and the rationale and relay those things that are harder to postulate against–storytelling, coupled with emotional appeal. Let's say you had a grandmother who made the most delicious homemade spaghetti sauce on the planet. And who took her chicken cutlets and pounded them real thin and placed them under a brick to flatten. And who rolled out her pasta by hand. And made every heartache you ever had go away with that one dish. Wouldn't it be hard for someone who loves you to turn down an opportunity to give you comfort after that story? Heck, it would be hard for someone who doesn't even know you to turn you down after hearing that.

But if your stories don't work, emotional appeal can work too. Telling the WHY you need what you need. The rationale and reasoning behind the request. Maybe you have had a really bad day and the carbs will lessen your despair. Maybe you got sick off seafood once and you still have post-traumatic stress after the experience. Maybe the restaurant you want to visit reminds you of the first time you met your significant other and you want to spend time remembering your own why.

These two tools are some of the most powerful ways to get others to see your point of view. You can come armed with data and logic and passion, but if someone is firm in their belief, it usually matters little when those are your only arguments. But relating to the heart and the soul and the emotions? Well, those are harder to argue with. Because feelings don't have reason. They don't have rationale. They just are. And if you can't argue with are, you really can't say no.

Of course, in the world of the workplace, food choices are often the least important battle. Not always (I can tell some pretty deep and dark moments surrounding food) but leaders usually face controversial decisions with higher implications. Passions may be more embedded and harder to sway. Even the best storyteller may need a little help. And that is where things like data, facts, historical context, and good old-fashioned negotiation and give and take come into play. Oftentimes we can get close to consensus but get stuck on the minute. Using the stories and the emotions for these smaller contentions will help come to resolutions.

And it is forever important to remember, your way is not the only way and may not be the best way. While you may be trying to insert the influence, you must also allow yourself to be influenced. Someone's story or emotional appeal may, in fact, be more important than your own. You may be willing to bend and lean into theirs for the betterment of the greater good and your relationship with that person. You may just want some seafood after all!

Finally, there are some things outside of your control. There are some things you literally cannot change, no matter how emotional you get or how many stories you can tell. Wasting time worrying about, planning around, or concerning yourself with these external factors is pointless and unnecessary. Identify what you can control and use your influence to change those things that can be changed.

Virtual Spark Applications:

- Be over the top with emotion and conviction. You need to put on a show to reach across the virtual landscape.
- Grab their attention with video messaging, music, and graphics. The virtual world is filled with boring emails. Do something different to create excitement.
- Be honest and transparent, even in virtual space. Show your feelings. Discuss your thoughts. Overshare. Allowing people the opportunity to know you will create a feeling of loyalty and the desire to assist in any way possible.

CREATING HAPPINESS WITH A
SPARK

ONCE UPON A TIME there was a leader who took her team to the most magical place on earth for some team building and professional learning. She understood the importance of experiencing big things together as a team and understood the need to believe in magic within the difficult departments these ladies were responsible for overseeing. So, she created a well-laid plan to ensure the team experienced the fun, were filled with yummy sustenance, and could believe in the power of infinite possibilities.

But you know that saying about best laid plans…. well, even in the most magical place on earth, plans can go **POOF!** Crumble! And while in line for a particularly fun experience, the experience kept "getting delayed". And so, what should have been a 7:00 pm dinner pick up got pushed back to 7:30 pm.

Which was fine. Except………. the fireworks……. the most magical part of the whole day, was happening at 8:15 pm. AND having the best seat possible to view the show required securing a place to sit by 7:30 pm.

Herein lay the dilemma. Eat and miss the show? Or send

10 hungry ladies out to watch a magical experience on an empty belly? Neither felt right to the leader of the group, so a master plan was hatched on the spot.

They would divide and conquer! A team of five traveled to find the best possible viewing location, while the other five waited on the food and would deliver it to the location "picnic style,". Now on paper, this seems like an easy and reasonable situation. Except when you consider the following details:

1. The food was not baggable. We are talking trays of fajitas, tubs of sour cream, dishes of lettuce and tomato.
2. The drinks did not have lids. Picture Diet Cokes and lemonades filled to the rims.
3. The restaurant was about as far away from the viewing spot as possible.
4. The most magical place on earth was filled with magic seekers. All descending on one centralized location to experience the magic in the skies.
5. And finally, time was ticking away because the fireworks do not wait for the meals to be cooked and then delivered.

A challenge, right? One that might seem impossible. One that might make someone think they have no choice but to choose. Except, when you have a team of ladies filled with determination that understand and believe in the mission and know they can accomplish the impossible with teamwork and dedication, the impossible can happen.

The team of five found the perfect spot. They spread themselves out on the cold concrete and subjected them-selves to bumps and bruises from passerby's strollers and wheelchairs and backpacks to ensure the perfect spot, with room for all, was secured.

Meanwhile, the food team devised a plan, on the spot, that included surrounding the drink tray carrier almost as a shield and navigating the streets and the people with constant commentary ("go left!" "Watch the curb!" "don't laugh or you will drop the tray!"). I won't lie. I know there were moments where we all just wanted to find a spot to sit and call the spot getters to us and just watch the fireworks from wherever we landed. But collectively we cheered each other to the literal finish line.

And then, sitting amongst the masses, we ate. And laughed. And celebrated the moment. The win. And when the skies lit up with fireworks and music played and people cheered, we were rewarded with sparkles in the heavens. Despite being surrounded by thousands, it felt like they were shining just for us.

Leading requires a goal. Leading requires risks. Leading requires outside of the box thinking. Leading requires relying on others when you can't do it all. Leading requires letting others take charge. Leading requires teamwork. Only when you do the above can you beat impossible odds to reach your goals. And when you do that, you will most certainly be rewarded with a little bit of magic.

Virtual Spark Applications:

- You don't need fireworks and Diet Cokes. In fact, those things are hard (but not impossible) to do virtually. But you do need intentionality and planning. Create opportunities for connection unrelated to work. This can be at the start of a virtual meeting or a standalone event.

- Don't be afraid to step out of the virtual box. You CAN meet in person with some planning and notification. In fact, this is necessary to truly create cohesion amongst a team.
- While planning is great and crucial, know you cannot control it all. Be sure to go with the flow. Let others lead the way and organize virtual get togethers, fun, magic, without your guidance. Give and encourage those in your charge to do their own magic-making with the collaboration tools available and know you don't have to lead it all.

CELEBRATE GOOD TIMES,
COME ON!

WHEN I WAS EXECUTIVE DIRECTOR, I had to plan a welcome back celebration for the return of a beloved colleague. His return deserved a special celebration, as he had basically built the school, having been involved since day one!

Sparky Alicia immediately got to planning. There was a surprise announcement, walk up music, and "cool sparks" which are basically really big sparklers controlled by a remote control. I mean, what could go wrong?!?!

Well, I tell you what went wrong....... Alicia almost set the Chief Academic Officer on fire. That is what went wrong. She got hold of the remote control and at the most inopportune moment, lit up the stage, with the CAO standing right next to them. Talk about too much spark!

And yet, while that moment of celebration was a potential dumpster fire, no pun intended, that celebration in and of itself led to a common language and rallying cry for the rest of that school year. It was used as an analogy for everything going well to everything going wrong at the school. Sometimes, celebrations can live on for long after they end and truly create a cultural moment.

I am not saying you should aim to replicate this disaster. But I am saying that what may appear to be a frivolous prop or silly practice, can actually be the thing to build community and relationship for the long run. Take the chance and buy the sound system. Get the chocolate fountain. Create a hype video. These shared experiences will live long past whatever you are celebrating and become the stories that bind!

How do celebrations apply to the day to day?

Oh, does a Spark like a good party. And a theme around a good party? What?! What?! But sometimes (and oh my goodness I cannot even believe I am about to write this), there can be too much celebrating. ShUdDeR!!!!!!

You know how everybody is complaining all the time about all the trophies? And how we are raising a generation that believes they must be rewarded for everything? Well, I am a prime-time contributor to that problem. And not just with the baby generation but with all the generations.

You see, I love me a good competition. It brings about teamwork and results. And when you incentivize something, it tends to get attention. But what happens when you incentivize everything? Two things tend to happen. 1. People EXPECT to be rewarded for every single aspect of their job. And 2. People become numb to the rewards.

Because of my predisposition to celebrating, I faced a backlash to this during my time as a school leader. Our administrative team loved to reward just about everything with time off. If you won the staff trivia contest you got time off. If you reached a department goal, the entire department got time off. And if you took on extra tasks/responsibilities, you were rewarded with, you guessed it, time off. Very quickly, people had earned so much time off they couldn't use it. And began to complain about that. It was quickly recognized we had to do something different, but this had become so ingrained in all we did that there was backlash to our attempt to stop the time off train.

Changing that culture is HARRRRRRRRRRRRD-DDDDDDDD. And, sadly, self-inflicted. PLEASE heed my warning and be sure your rewards and incentives are for those that truly go above and beyond and are used sparingly.

And then there are alllll the days and groups and moments that some feel need to be recognized and acknowledged. You know things like....

Let's celebrate staff with brown eyes who are five feet tall and have an August birthday.

Let's celebrate You Were Born in the 80s and Grew Up in Idaho Day.

Let's celebrate all the Assistants to the Regional Directors. I joke.... sort of.

Because all you must do is scroll through social media and see that someone is celebrating their dog on dog day or their son on son day or their in-law or aunt or grandparent.

And while recognizing groups and giving shout outs is a wonderful way to show appreciation, even with the best laid plan, you will forget about a subpopulation. And then the recognition becomes hurt feelings and accusations of favoring one group over another. A dangerous path to travel on.

Instead of whole group recognition, it is far better to encourage frequent and singular praise tied to a desired behavior. Gather a list of all your employees and find ways to individually recognize them throughout the year. Maybe you send them a handwritten note. Maybe you call their names out at a staff meeting. Maybe you send flowers to their home. Finding and recognizing the good for specifics will have far bigger impact than celebrating a specific group just because there is a day designated for them.

Finally, be sure to make opportunities for staff to celebrate with each other. Have virtual platforms and ways in which employees can recognize each other. Set calendar reminders for your whole staff to take time to show appreciation. Make celebration a part of your culture, particularly the type that comes from within, as opposed to top down. Allow committees to plan the ways in which the whole staff will recognize and celebrate each other. And then gauge the effectiveness of each endeavor frequently.

Lee Cockerell, an executive at Disney, once said "I never had thoughts of I'm getting way too much appreciation, recognition and encouragement," and while that is true, the ways in which we are giving those things CAN be too much. Find ones that work, use them often and revisit their effectiveness frequently to maximize all your celebrating and all your efforts.

Virtual Spark Applications:

- Oh, this is SO EASY to do virtually! There are various celebration platforms that you can promote and encourage people to use when the mood strikes them. You can also create calendar reminders to help drive the celebration train forward.
- Remember the creating magic chapter? Well, you also need to create celebrations and traditions. Find time to call the team together to recognize greatness. This can be done monthly or quarterly but needs to be consistent and scheduled.
- Be sure to individually celebrate as well. Send snail mail (yes, pens and paper and stamps still work in the virtual world). Craft a complimentary email. Send that happy text.

- And set your own calendar reminder to look for the things that need to be celebrated and follow up often.

LAUGHTER IS THE BEST
MEDICINE

Quick! Think back to your favorite work memory. And not your most accomplished work memory. And not the memory of you walking out of a job you hated. But the memory that you still talk about.... the "remember the time so and so did something with someone?!?!" I would guarantee that memory either involves copious amounts of laughter OR brings you copious amounts of laughter.

I was blessed to lead for over a decade with people that value laughter. And so, I am blessed to have thousands of "favorite" memories, and just about all of them either involved or now bring big, loud belly laughs. We have faced many huge challenges, namely growing a teeny tiny public school, on the literal forefront of virtual education, into the largest public school in the state and one of the best performing virtual schools in the nation. With that growth and with that spotlight comes pretty challenging situations. Budgets and personnel issues and state and federal mandates (designed for the brick-and-mortar world, no less) add all kinds of pressure and stress. It would be very easy to live in a constant state of serious despair. I mean, no one would have blamed us. But instead, we found the humor in all the things…..the time we had to discipline an employee outside a bowling alley, when we lugged graduation cookies all over the hottest city in the country praying they didn't crack, the wet blanket hanging on a chain link fence that almost got some of us fired, holding a meeting in a hotel lobby while a stranger slept on a chair in the middle of us, the time I sent some high school students wine tumblers as a thank you, etc. etc. etc. etc. These events not only brought us to tears, but they also brought us closer together. And through laughter you build camaraderie, which brings greater chances of success.

While it is easy to find humor in the silly and fun, it is just as important to insert and utilize humor in the serious and the tough. I once had to give a pretty dire state of the school address to a staff of 260. In it, I talked about budget cuts and department moves and the need for people to step up and take on more. None of those are topics that incite laughter. However, I found ways to bring levity. I knew I had to. While I delivered very serious and important news with facts and not so fun details, I also found ways to make the room laugh. And at the end of those words, the thanks and the appreciation were palpable. The staff was grateful for my honesty and felt good about the words. I know that some of it had to do with my delivery and a big part of that was ensuring it was delivered with levity.

You can also find time to weave humor into frustration. I had an employee crying to me about some negative feedback she had received on a staff survey. I gave her the space to describe what was happening and why she felt the way she did. I listened and sympathized, which was of utmost importance in the moment. But then, we ended with me telling her to take that feedback and throw it in a firepit and watch it go up in flames. And she started laughing. And I started laughing. And together we ended a very difficult moment with her recognizing the absurdity of some of the feedback. It is a moment that continues to unite us to this day.

Don't be afraid to laugh about the tough stuff or the fun stuff or the serious stuff or the annoying stuff. Find the humor wherever and whenever you can. It will not only help bond you with those around you, but it will also truly make your days that much better, and shouldn't that be what it is all about anyway??

Virtual Spark Applications:

- Memes! Silly graphics! Gif yourself (yes this is a thing). Let your silly side shine. Virtual spaces do not need to be a boring reality. Allow the fun in and use it often.
- Make frivolity a part of the culture. Enter the karaoke contest at the leadership retreat. Schedule a bake-off challenge the next time you meet. Bring a board game to the next face to face meeting. SCHEDULE the laughs and they will come and then come often without the need for a calendar invite.
- Share the funny things that happen to you and encourage others to do the same. Even if that "takes up meeting time." This creates a virtual space people want to join and look forward to, rather than avoiding.

MASTERING THE ART OF
COMMUNICATION WITH A SPARK

A STORY of what NOT to do:

As a school leader, I received many "urgent" needs to be completed ASAP, requests from various entities. The federal government. That state department of education. The district. Our Education Management Organization. And I almost always knew to act with caution before jumping. What appeared to be "urgent" almost always had a long runway of opportunity for completion. Therefore, I would take the time to review the request, think through the best plan for implementation, craft appropriate communication to the required parties, and then start the process.

96.3% of the time.

Because I am human and because, sometimes, I fall into the "urgent" trap, there have been occasions where I fired off incomplete and undetailed information before creating a plan for implementation.

This happened most recently when our school's school report card rating was hanging in the balance. The district sent me an urgent document that detailed the need for all our students, staff, and caretakers to complete a survey to get

ALICIA HUGHES

points on the school report card. This task was an easy do it or don't. The kind of "low hanging fruit" you don't ignore when working to demonstrate compliance and success. There was also a fairly short window in which to get 6300 students, 270 staff members and over 10,000 caretakers to comply. Now, that seemed urgent and important to convey ASAP.

However, I knew better. I knew waiting before writing and, more importantly, waiting before hitting send was crucial. This was not a yes or no answer. This required clear directions for where to go, how to log in, and how to answer questions designed for a brick and mortar setting in the virtual space. And yet, I threw together an URGENT PLEASE READ NOW message with very little content and lots of exclamation marks!

And then, in poured the questions. Where do I go? How do I answer certain questions? What is my password? What happens if my username is not in the system? Etc. Etc. Etc.

And what did I do in this situation? Did I hit pause and craft a clear document with detailed directions? Did I make a recording that demonstrated the answers to the most common questions? Did I phone a friend? Nope! Sure didn't! I committed communication chaos once again! By quickly crafting another all-staff email that attempted to haphazardly answer the most common questions. Which led to even MORE questions to which I did not have the answers.

As you work to craft ANY communication, and this applies to both written and verbal, remember to pause. Remember to think. And remember to be sure the words you share are logical and appropriate and as clear as possible. Otherwise, you will spend many more hours cleaning up what is unnecessary and avoidable confusion.

The Spark's Biggest Challenge to Crafting Communication:

Common Advice: Clear is kind. Details are great. Thinking before speaking is important.

Blech. Yuck. Gross…. Are those the first things that came to your head? If so, my Spark Friend, know you are in good company.

Sparks like to act fast and furious. They like to quickly jump into things and solve problems in record time. They often neglect details and specifics in the name of rapid response.

And while this quality can be great in critical, must-solve-immediately situations, it is often a downfall in the day to day. Because there are very few must-solves in the life of a leader and more often long-term projects and goals that require intentional roll out.

How does a Spark be sure to think before responding and reacting? Well, instituting the rule of 24. And that means…. waiting at least 24 hours to respond to anything that needs more than a yes or no response. Anything that needs to be communicated with any bit of detail and thought needs at least 24 hours to marinate and simmer.

And even if you are not a spark, think about how many times you have reviewed a conversation or email you have been a part of and wished you could have a redo? Probably just about every time. I wish I had or had not said that. Or if only I had phrased it this way.

Waiting 24 hours allows for many things to occur. Most importantly, it allows you, the responder, to fully think on the question/problem and decide how you would like to respond. If you will be discussing the situation live (this includes phone calls) it allows you time to practice what you want to say and get all points conveyed clearly. If you are responding in writing, EVEN BETTER! There is a delete button and a spell checker :) You can write whatever moves you and then go back and edit to fit your tone and needs.

But how about those things that don't require immediate answers? Policies, procedures, directives and instructions? Well, my spark friend, again not what you want to hear but.... DETAILS DETAILS DETAILS! Don't assume the reader knows the answer. Don't assume the reader will utilize common sense. Anticipate every question and concern and try to verbalize the answers to the best of your ability. Clear. Is. Kind.

That being said.... get ready for the contradiction......a Spark's arch nemesis! Be sure not to use too many words. There is nothing worse than a multiple page document with long-winded explanations that truly could have been written in four sentences. There is nothing worse than something being overly complicated. Nothing worse than something that leads to more questions and more confusion.

Wondering how to balance both? Too much info with too little? Here is a trick I use............give the process/procedure/directive to someone outside of your organization. Ask them if it makes sense. Ask them if they understand. Ask them if it is too short, too long or just right. This person could be your significant other or your child or your best friend or your mom. Anyone who can review and give advice as an outsider looking in. You can also ask someone within your organization who may be in a different department or location. This helps with clarity around the specifics.

Finally, always be **you** in your communication.

Remember, while you need to be clear and detailed, you also need to ensure the receiver hears your voice and understands your intent, whether in writing or in person. So many times, people misunderstand what we say or what we write because they misinterpret our tone. Being crystal clear and intentional with word choice is often the key to avoiding confusion. When people know you are upset, they may work harder to change. When people know you are being firm, they will be sure to toe the line. And when people know you are being lighthearted, they won't fear retribution or lash outs. Do whatever it takes to convey your true feelings, whether in words or voice. THAT is what people remember and THAT is what gets the strongest reaction. And you, my spark friend, have the feeling conveying thing down pat!

Virtual Spark Applications:

- There are many options in which to communicate. Instant messaging, texts, emails, phone calls, Slack, Discord…. The list is infinite. Be intentional with the ways in which you communicate. Pick one platform and stick with it.
- Have communication norms. It is far too easy to send things out after hours or on weekends and holidays. Stick to communication during business hours only unless it is an emergency that cannot wait.
- Reevaluate norms and platforms frequently. Implement new processes and procedures when necessary. Since remote work is in isolation, having operating communication systems that allow for efficiency and collaboration is key to a strong organizational culture and output.

SUNSHINE AND RAINBOWS
ALWAYS

TOXIC POSITIVITY. The newest buzz word when you want to complain about something. Yep. Let's find a way to make positivity negative!

And I get it. Believe me. There are times I am throwing up glitter while shooting a confetti cannon and tap dancing on top of a glow in the dark table that I think.........

"Hmmmm did I go one piece of confetti too far?"

"Am I annoying the ever-loving poop out of people?"

And I will rein it in. But "toxic positivity's" definition is a lot more than one piece of confetti too much....

Toxic positivity is the pressure to only display positive emotions, suppressing the negative ones. It makes sadness and frustration taboo, leading to isolation and unhealthy coping mechanisms.

That I get. If someone comes to me and has had a horrible event occur, I recognize how terrible it would feel if someone negated that emotion and minimized it, so that the person felt ashamed. I also understand there are some that live in a positive bubble and refuse to prepare for danger due to the belief that everything will be ok. Yes, that makes total sense. And is terrible. And truly the opposite of positivity!

But many are beginning to use this term in a negative way. To beat down anyone who tries to look on the bright side. By combating those sunshine and rainbowers with Negative Nelly vibes.

And as someone who lives in extremes, I can usually see both sides. If you are a glass half empty person, it might be hard to get on board the half full mindset. If you have had a string of bad situations occur, it might be annoying to be around someone who seems to be excessively happy. And if you live in concrete, data-based reality, it may be hard to believe in the hopes and dreams of the anything is possible!

How to balance? How to not be TOO positive? Too hopeful? Too happy? If that is your way here is what I say…………

Do. Not. Change. For real. Be true to you! If you like to bounce through life happy and jolly, filled with glitter and shine, EMBRACE THAT! I doubted this for 2.2 seconds recently when I was called toxically positive. Then I took a deep look at my practices and realized the term was not being applied properly. I am annoyingly positive. And maybe loud and bright and uber optimistic. But I know to sympathize and be realistic in the face of sadness and adversity….

This quote, from Amy Weatherly, is something I believe in this with all my being:

Live your life with as much light as you can and if it burns other people's eyes, so be it! Toos them some cheap sunglasses and keep shining away.

And so, ALWAYS be you! If you want to be glass half empty, AWESOME! If you want to believe that negativity will get you places, you do you. But I will never apologize for happiness or joy or cheerfulness. I will sparkle and shine 'til the day I die. #Sunshineandrainbows4evah!

Virtual Spark Applications:

- What I love most about the virtual space is the ability to take a breath and think before reacting. Don't respond immediately to situations in which you might feel negatively. Take the time to fume and then respond with kindness and positivity.
- Find all the positive memes, gifs, clips, images you can and use them in communication often. Heck, put a quote in your email signature. Or screen share a positive quip to start a meeting.
- Kill 'em with kindness. Write the happy email to someone who never seems to be. Answer vinegar with sugary sweet. Smile on webcam. Exude positivity in every interaction both asynchronous and synchronous. It is contagious!

THE BURNING CHAPTERS

*HOW TO ENSURE YOUR SPARK IS
CONTAINED WHILE BURNING BRIGHTLY*

YOUR MOST IMPORTANT RESOURCE–PEOPLE!

THINK for a minute about your favorite restaurant/shop/hotel. And think about the reason you love it so much. It probably has little to do with the product you purchase there or the experience you received, but rather the way it made you FEEL. Do you instantly feel happy upon entry? Valued? Important? Probably all those things and more. You are not apathetic or angry or sad when there. In fact, you seek that place out when you ARE feeling any of those things. Positive feelings are strong motivators to a return investment.

The same is true for your organization. Your people should WANT to be at work. They should feel mostly positive feelings around the work they do. And while work is, well, work, they should choose your organization over the many other options available to them. They should come ready to do whatever is necessary for your organization because it is such a point of pride and enjoyment to them.

Getting people to want to be working at your organization is really not rocket science. There isn't a secret ingredient. And it really isn't hard. It is treating others like you would like to be treated. It is working to give them enjoyment and satisfaction in their experience. It is seeking them out to give them the best customer experience possible to ensure they are a return client. It is making them want others to be a part of this place and telling the world about the great things going on.

I recently had two very differing experiences at two food establishments within a 24-hour period. Both were similar in that they were small, locally owned businesses that offered a limited lunch menu that could be prepared quickly to either dine in or take with you.

At the first location, I walked to the counter and the young lady standing at the register looked at me like she wanted to slap me. Hmmmmm...I certainly didn't feel welcome. But in my typical way, I attempted banter and small talk in hopes I would brighten HER day. That was NOT happening. My inner dialogue reminded me that she may have been facing a horrific personal challenge and was just trying to get by, so I gave up trying to be cheery and simply attempted to order. This person literally knew NOTHING about the menu, rang up the WRONG order (and it wasn't anything complicated) and then did not even acknowledge nor apologize to me for her lack of information or her errors. To say I will never again grace that establishment is an understatement.

The next day, at a different establishment, I was immediately greeted by the young man behind the register. He was full of information on the menu and unabashedly honest ("That sauce is terrible! Choose this!"). He smiled, was patient, and kind throughout my time at the register. He also made a mistake with my order and forgot to include something, for which I had to return to the counter to receive. But he immediately apologized, offered to give me something complimentary, and showed genuine care and concern. To say I will highly recommend this establishment is an under-statement.

What makes these two people so different in their treat-ment of their roles? I would bet it comes from the top! I would bet the owner in the second scenario instills in them a sense of love and pride for their work. That the owner shows kindness, care, and concern for their employees, thus encouraging them to pay it forward. I am certain there was copious amounts of time training the young man at this establishment and very little time spent in care and expecta-tions in establishment one. It was apparent and obvious within seconds of entry.

Being people centric is about as easy as breathing for Sparks. People and relationships and togetherness are our faves. When people are NOT being cared for, that is when our sparks begin to fade. We fully understand the need to care for those in our charge for progress to be made. We know that if you invest in your staff, even if it takes time and resources, the payouts will be huge. But if this is not your go to here are some simple ways to make people your everything:

1. **Honor time.** Do not schedule over/require extra work/disrespect people's own time for your own. Your work is not more important than their work.
2. **You need to bend.** Just because someone's way is not your way, does not make it the wrong way. Allow for creativity and flexibility so long as the end goal is reached.
3. **Value and thank and appreciate**. Ensure that you recognize people for their contributions. Do not ignore or underscore hard work and dedication because "it is expected." Make it a habit to regularly

find time to thank and celebrate, even when it is "part of the job".

4. **Kindness**. Every time. Please. Thank you. Good morning. Goodbye. Simple, right? Your bad day, your bad mood, your bad experience does not mean you get to unload on your team. Sometimes, you may need to dig deep to find kindness. Sometimes you may need to put on a show. However, consistently being kind forces others to do the same for those in which they serve.

5. **Be available.** Even when you are tired. Even when you are busy. Even when you are annoyed. Find a few minutes to listen. To chat. To be present. That small sacrifice will pay out in dividends.

The Flip Side..........

Sparks LOVE the people. They get their energy from the people. People are EvErYtHiNg! Putting people first might be a weakness for them. It might work against them at times, and it might hurt the organization in some way. Sparks want everyone to be happy and filled with fun and fulfillment and may feel pulled to put people's needs and desires above the common good.

How to combat this?

1. **Set boundaries**. You do not need to give in to every question/whim/request. You do not need to immediately solve the problems. You do not need to make accommodations for every request. You CAN sympathize. You CAN provide resources to help in situations. You CAN be available to listen. You do not ever need to bend so far to one that the rest are put in precarious situations.

2. **Allow others to figure things out without assistance.** Give space and time for problem solving. This will help them grow in the long run and make your organization that much better.

3. **Ensure you know where your line in the sand stands.** Don't go over it. Consistently stick to it. Because if you go too far with one, you will have to go too far with the next. And the next. And the next.

4. **Find your tribe and surround yourself with them.** If you are in a position of leadership, there MUST be a bit of separation from your direct reports. You cannot vent/confide/share too much with the world at large. Make sure your leadership team is tight and supportive, as it truly is lonely at the top, and for Sparks, there is nothing worse than loneliness!

5. **Too much CAN be bad.** All the talking, the gushing, the sparkiness? You can go too far. It can be distracting. It can be annoying. Be sure that your words and your enthusiasms are appropriate for given situations. Otherwise, you go from being someone people love to have around to someone people wish to avoid.

Virtual Spark Applications:

- The boundary thing is key here. Because in the virtual space, there is no door to shut to indicate your lack of availability. Emails/texts/Instant messages come whenever the staff member sees the need to reach out. And if you jump to answer immediately, staff will be conditioned to expect an immediate response every time. Don't jump every time called, and don't get distracted by the "urgent" requests.

- Stick to meeting times. Give space between meetings. Do not extend your meeting just because you are virtual. If more time is needed, find an additional time to meet. Don't just assume the people on the call can and want to extend.
- Respect other's time. Don't schedule meetings outside of the working day. Don't schedule over things like lunch or PTO. Don't send must read emails late in the evening. Work to make sure you are not taking advantage of the virtual nature of the job by going outside of the virtual lines.

WHAT MATTERS MOST AND HOW
DO WE GET THERE?

Deep, dark confession. Up until right this very moment, I had NO IDEA what the difference between a vision and a mission was. I thought they were synonyms (and quite frankly feel they should be…. I mean, why do you need TWO statements of what you want to do?!?) But I digress….

As I write this, I googled "what is the difference between vision and mission?" and came up with this:

A company's mission defines its business goals and the values it will embrace to achieve them. By contrast, a vision is a more abstract idea of how the organization intends to impact society. Rather than setting specific goals, it's something to strive for

Ummmmm…clear as mud, right?

Which leads me to a story….

Many moons ago, I was working with a group of leaders to create a vision and mission for our school. We spent HOURS upon HOURS upon HOURS writing sentences, striking out words, arguing over words. It was literally one of the most painful memories at a place I literally loved. And that was the biggest irony. We all loved our school so much, were so passionate about our work, and truly believed in the same cause....to help all kids learn. But we couldn't see the simplicity of that. We couldn't get past the words and the process to focus on what really mattered and we all knew to be true.... that we wanted to ensure all students learned.

And so, we stepped away, met a few more times, and finally half-heartedly agreed on two very long sentences, with lots of pretty words. And shortly after reading the very long sentences and placing them on websites and message boards and email signatures, I quickly forgot what they even said and moved on.... Lots of wasted time and effort and energy on something I literally never used or said again.

Fast forward a few years and the leadership team once again began a conversation around the need to revisit our vision and mission. This time, I was vocal in that we cannot spend weeks arguing over semantics. Our school leader at the time agreed. We quickly narrowed the words down to just a few.... Learning for All. And lightbulbs went off and relief filled the room. So simple, yet so true. So applicable to literally everything we did and so easy to remember and adapt.

Why do we make things so hard?? It should be simple to say what it is your organization stands for. Why you do what you do. It should not take a paragraph or a thesaurus or dictionary. It should be a rallying cry that easily comes from the heart.

Let's look at a few examples from large, well-known organizations:

Nike

Mission statement: Create groundbreaking sports innovations, make our products sustainable, build a creative and diverse global team, and make a positive impact in communities where we live and work.

Vision statement: Bring inspiration and innovation to every athlete* in the world. *If you have a body, you are an athlete.

Tesla

Mission statement: To create the most compelling car company of the 21st century by driving the world's transition to electric vehicles.

Vision statement: To accelerate the world's transition to sustainable energy.

TED

Mission statement: Spread ideas.

Vision statement: We believe passionately in the power of ideas to change attitudes, lives and, ultimately, the world.

Pretty simple and if you know the products, you are not at all surprised by the information above. It shouldn't be a secret. It shouldn't be difficult. It shouldn't be a surprise.

If you hate your vision and mission, don't know your vision and mission, or need a new vision and mission, remember these three things:

1. Keep it simple.
2. Keep it honest.
3. Make it meaningful.

Your employees must be on board. Your employees must easily remember the words. Your employees must see how their work contributes to the words. They must be able to tie it back to every single action and decision made. Only then does it truly impact your organization and only then does it become more than some pretty words on paper. And your organization definitely deserves more than that.

Virtual Spark Applications:

- This is something best done face to face. There are bound to be strong emotions and feelings around the decisions, so give plenty of time and space to allow for all thoughts to be shared.
- Build in breaks and fun during the process. This is heavy work and needs to be balanced with some light frivolity.
- Step away and come back. If you are doing this face to face, schedule a follow up virtual session if resolution is impossible. And if you start virtually but decide face to face is needed, never be afraid to give more time.

KEEP IT SIMPLE STUPID

You know how most people LOVE a bargain store? A shopping experience with all the randomly placed items and articles of clothing strewn about at discount prices. Y'all, I avoid those places like the plague. How about a diner with a menu 38 pages long with more appetizer choices than most grocery stores carry? Although I do love a good deal and different cuisine choices, I do not want to spend an exorbitant amount of time making a decision that ultimately has little to no impact on my life goals and objectives. I do not want to spend precious minutes searching to find a t-shirt in my size or king-sized bedspreads or choosing between a salad or a mozzarella stick or an egg roll or sliders. I would far rather walk into a place with a limited selection, grouped in appropriate ways, so that I can quickly find a sweater that will fit or readily decide on an entree as opposed to wasting time on the hunt.

What may seem dramatically out of character for a Spark such as myself is my strong distaste for too many options. Too many choices. Too much information. I think my desire to limit decision making possibilities comes from my strong love of fast action. If you must look through/read through/absorb copious amounts of information, the time spent on that process can drive me to madness, thus causing me to shut down and either blindly close my eyes and point to get the process moving OR turn it over to someone else.

When things are confusing or complicated, I get this feeling of claustrophobia. Isn't that weird? Things are SO VAST and SO WILD, yet I feel like the walls are closing in around me and I cannot escape. I literally shut down, feel like I am coming out of my skin, and have this burning desire to run as far away from the situation as humanly possible. Probably the one thing about leadership I hate the most. And if I feel this way, I am certain there are others on my team who share this sentiment.

I am not sure why leaders feel the need to overcomplicate things, but we do. I think sometimes it comes from a place of control. We want everyone to be on the same page and so we spell out every single action step with every single possible scenario, thus causing overwhelm.

It may also come from the piling on process. And by that I mean, you start with a relatively simple idea. You get feedback, so things get added. And then, with time, more situations occur to cause necessary changes. And so, what started small, grows into something much larger and unmanageable.

As leaders, we have an obligation to make our processes and procedures as easy to find and understand as the quest to find an item in a store or a selection for dinner at the diner. We should always be chunking the information and organizing it in a way that no one must sort through sweaters to find the shorts. We need to provide the information needed to do the job and do it well, but not so much information that the directions to the goal become lost in the words. Keep it simple, stupid is a saying and a best practice for a reason. The more you add, the harder it becomes to keep up with.

While bargain shopping and diner dining is a wonderful opportunity, it is not a place that allows a walk in, get it and go experience. And while variety is the spice of life, variety in the workplace is not an effective way in which to operate. Do yourselves a favor and leave the random, overstimulating menu full of options to the diners and the bargain stores and keep the specific and concise for your daily practices. I promise, no one will leave to go look for a bigger variety of choices.

Virtual Spark Applications:

- The virtual world is vast. Copious amounts of platforms and information and possibilities exist. It is so easy to get lost in the cyber world. Find a few platforms/communication tools and stick to them. Don't keep adding and adding and adding.
- Google docs are amazing things. Allowing everyone to collaborate and share is crucial to organizational success. However, Google docs get lost in the Google world without clear organization. Be sure to have naming metrics, folders, and systems in place to keep up with it all.
- Don't make things more complicated due to physical distance. If there is confusion, reach out and ask the person who has the answers. Don't wait 'til your next meeting. If you don't ask for clarity, you are assured to make things more difficult not only for yourself, but anyone who needs your assistance.

NOT TOO TIGHT NOT TOO LOOSE
BUT JUST RIGHT

Oh, my Spark Friends…. Let's be real here. Being tight about anything is not usually your jam. You have BIG and EXCITING ideas, but when you set them out into the universe, you simply hope that everyone knows exactly what to do to achieve your vision (I mean, why can't people read your mind??). Details, shmetails. You have an end goal. You know where you WANT to go and you have an idea of how to get there, but you hope that everyone just "does whatever is needed so that the goal is reached,". And, in the beginning, when everyone is working on something, you feel good. Until you look around and see the things they are working on are counterproductive or inefficient or just plain wrong. You actually HAD tight expectations, you just got so carried away in the end goal that you forgot to share those. You know the bare bones of what MUST be done, and you know what is up to interpretation, yet you weren't actually tight about those details, only the end result.

You live in the world of the loose. Even when there are crystal clear expectations and processes (which are usually someone else's creation). You believe that everything will fall into place. The big idea will be carried through, even when there are bumps and setbacks along the way. Your enthusiasm and positive belief will also be your downfall.

How to make the main thing tight and ensure you aren't so loose it all falls apart?

Let's use an analogy that most of my sparkiest friends can relate to…. party planning! Whoop whoop!

If you have done this a time or two, you know that you must make some decisions, and usually your planning goes something like this.

BIG DREAMS! You got confetti and DJs and ice sculptures and balloon arches and cupcakes galore in your vision. But then…. whomp whomp whomp…. The reality that you have an actual budget to contend with sets in, so choices need to be made. You review all your options and quickly decide the must haves for this event to be the best ever and what you can skimp on and still get the most bang for your buck. Maybe music is CRUCIAL to the event at hand and the biggest part of your budget goes to the DJ, while you opt for the lowest tier of passed hors d'oeuvres. Or you determine you need a WOW factor when your guests first arrive, so you dedicate a big portion of funds to all things location and decor and opt to stream tunes over the provided AV system. You see where I am going with this? You quickly determine where you are going to be TIGHT and where you can be LOOSE, yet still achieve the dream.

As you know, most of your work as a leader is NOT in party planning, sadly. But you can utilize this mindset as you determine what needs to be tight and what can be loose.

I have found a chart to be useful in this exercise, as this does not come naturally to me. Something like this:

What MUST happen consistently?

What can be emphasized but implemented with flexibility?

What really doesn't matter?

And then I list the action steps necessary in each column. With the mindset that when I convey the process/procedure/plan to staff, I will ensure I clearly communicate the first column as required, no ifs ands or buts and still emphasize the middle column and maybe don't say too much about the third.

Back to party planning, just to show an example of how this would go. Let's say I am planning the back-to-school meeting for my school and I want to ensure we kick off the year with excitement and enthusiasm and hope and positivity. I want our staff to feel appreciated and valued and loved. I want them to remember this meeting all year and be able to call it back to their memories when they are feeling downtrodden and hopeless. Here is where I would prioritize my efforts:

What MUST happen consistently?

What can be emphasized but implemented with flexibility?

What really doesn't matter?

- FUN! We need to convey a light, spirited exciting vibe.
- Positive messaging around school goals and objectives for the year
- Welcoming of new staff
- Celebrations from last school year
- Whole school announcements
- Back to school processes and procedures (this will be done in department time)
- Food
- Seating charts
- Venue fanciness
- Nitty gritty policies and procedures

And from there I begin to build out this dream…. first conveying it to my leadership team, so they know where to be tight and where to be loose and then to the staff. And, when decisions need to be made about the event, I return to this chart and see where this decision falls in the grand scheme of the goal. Finally, I share with the staff and set the tone and expectations right from the start.

While no plan is foolproof and sometimes things will get muddy, it is always important to step back and remember what the main thing is. And, when you have it in your head and on paper and have put it out into the universe for all to hear, well, it makes it that much easier to clearly see it and tighten your grip on it. And the other pulls will start to fade away.

Virtual Spark Applications:

- Use the charts above! And ask others to do the same. Make it a collaborative endeavor that can be added to throughout the project or process.
- Find staff that LOVE the details and ask them to help. Get yourself a notetaker as you wax poetic on your big idea. And then allow those that love the small things to present you with their interpretation of your process that can be edited to share with the masses.
- Embrace organizational tools and platforms that make idea generating and sharing a natural part of your process. AND call on AI to help get you started if needed.

HOLDING FEET TO THE FIRE TO
KEEP THE FIRE BURNING

"Do. Your. Job." --Dr. Amanda Ebel.

Quoting one of my former "bosses" here because if everyone did this consistently, we would not need this chapter. If employees simply did what they were employed to do and did it with their highest and best effort, accountability would be completely unnecessary, as all would be accountable to themselves. What a magical place that would be!

But, alas, this is not the case. Accountability measures need to be put into place and followed frequently and consistently.

However, there are different levels of accountability, so it is crucial to know your staff and use the measure that best fits the employee.

Here are some examples of accountability measures frequently utilized given the situation and employee:

The slacker support: These supports are designed for the employees that oftentimes cannot uphold the basic tenets of their role. Perhaps they are late every day. Perhaps they miss deadlines. Perhaps they forget important meetings. They violate the most basic, most understandable, and therefore, most enforceable, procedures. These situations and these supports are the most frustrating, yet easiest to assist with.

After an initial conversation about the identified problems, (most assuredly with support from your Human Resources department and all necessary documentation), ask the employee for their ideas as to how we can ensure they have the help they need to prevent future infractions. If they do not have ideas OR if their ideas are too minimal for the infraction, solutions can include:

- daily check-ins with their manager each morning and afternoon to discuss what needs to be completed and then what has been completed.
- A mentor system might also be useful to be less big brother and more supportive.
- An end of week meeting to review successes and discuss continued areas for improvement.

The overachiever support: This support is the exact opposite of the one above. This employee continuously goes above and beyond. You never have to wonder if they are going to finish a project, follow up with a customer, or show up to a mandatory event. But you do have to wonder if they are going too far outside of their lane. Are they doing other's work? Are they spending time working on things outside their scope? Are they working long hours, thus risking a future burn out?

These employees need to be reined in and reminded that there must be a work-life balance and a work-work balance to ensure they continue to operate at their highest and best. With this support, spontaneity is key. Check to see when they arrive and leave each day and gently remind them of the start and stop times. Observe where they are spending their time…are they involved in all optional committees and groups? Are they volunteering to help others? Are they spinning their wheels to send "ideas" and "thoughts" to departments and groups in which they have little to no interaction? Collect specific examples of these actions and share them with them in a safe and gentle conversation. Acknowledge all their work comes from a place of good but show how those continued actions can negatively impact the organization. Discuss the WHY behind why these behaviors must cease immediately and discuss the fact that if they continue, a disciplinary action may occur. Typically, this threat alone will pause an overachiever in their tracks. But, if it does not, stay true to your word and course by monitoring, documenting and then delivering that discipline should the behaviors continue.

The gray area support: This is your hardest support to implement. Hence the word gray. These are the employees that don't necessarily break established policies yet break culture. Maybe they don't act completely professionally, yet not enough to need a disciplinary conversion. Maybe they do the bare minimum consistently and occasionally less than. How do you support them in areas that aren't clearly defined?

The key here is building your relationship with them. Find out what makes them tick. What motivates them. What will inspire them to live more outside the gray and closer to expectations. Once that relationship is built, you can safely discuss your concerns. In this case, my Spark friend, your greatest strength will become your best tool. The power of persuasion and influence and inspiration will be the support you can most utilize. AND if this does not change the behaviors, it may be time to persuade and influence this employee into seeking other options. If they cannot conform to expectation clearly and consistently, they may need help finding a place in which they can.

Virtual Spark Applications:

- In some ways, it is easier to monitor virtually. There are platforms that can show productivity, group project platforms that give detailed accounts of who is doing what and when (think of Google's history tracking options in the Doc App), and even quick check-ins through messaging apps to ask for updates in the moment.
- Like with everything in the virtual world, accountability takes planning. Because you will not be walking by someone's office or chatting with them at the water cooler, you must actively seek out data and information to ensure things are moving forward as planned.
- Ask for frequent check-ins either asynchronously (emails or project summaries) or during scheduled live meetings. And follow up frequently if needed.

CH-CH-CH-CHANGES

ALL RIGHT. About to start with something you are not gonna like.

You gotta go slow to go fast.

Did you just throw up in your mouth a little bit? Break out into a cold sweat? Hate every single letter in each word combo? Yep. Me. Too.

Us Sparks like to go ffffffffffff-faaaaaaaaaaaaaaaaaaaaaasssssssssssssssstttttttttttttt. We want to blow things up and watch the flames flicker. We need big, loud, obvious impacts. Anything slow and methodical is tortuous.

But after a decade in leadership, I have finally learned to embrace a very simple truth.... You gotta look and plan before you jump. Baby steps are the best steps. You need to have all your things with you, PLUS be looking out ahead to see what might get in your way before blindly going forward. Taking the time to adequately prepare is going to be the best method every time or else you are going to be continuously stopping and starting to gather what you need.

But oooooooooooooohhhhhhhhhhhh boy is that HARD for Sparks. Very, very, very hard. You know it to be true, but there is always a loud voice cheering you along saying..........
but this time might be the time it all just works out. This time might be the time you don't need the parachute and the life jacket and the wetsuit before jumping off the cliff. This time you might land smoothly and safely and just start swimming to the finish line. That voice will be there. It is **your** loud voice, after all. But learning to quiet it will be the best thing you can do for yourself and, more importantly, your organization.

This is where you GOTTA lean into those quieter voices in your head. The things you know to be true and rely on in an emergency situation. And the reason you need to change is because, well, there is an emergency. Because if you don't change, great disaster will await. No one (no one with a bit of sense anyway) changes just to change. Change is the result of an identified need for the greater good. Utilize your best people that do these things well to rely on. And don't worry, you will have a huge (and dare I say, most important) part to play where your skill set will be most effective and useful.

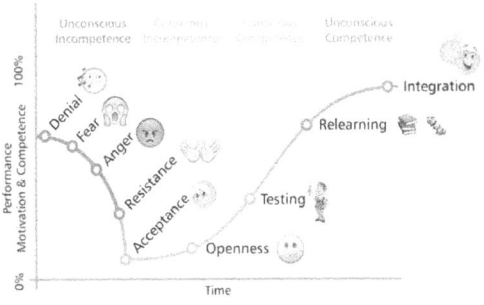

You see those emojis up there on the left? Any time

there's a new initiative, process, procedure, heck, even just a hint of an idea around change, people are going to react negatively. But my spark friend, this is when your super-power of making things exciting and acceptable and positive and good comes into play. You will build excitement and acceptance through your words, through your influence, through your passion. You will move people through the negative stages and get them to accept and be open to change. They will follow you, even when in doubt, even in fear, because you are going to make them see that this change is necessary, and this change will be great.

And then you take a step back. You find the people that love to create the processes. Love to create the procedures. Love all the details and organization surrounding this. You continue to be your spark self by constantly reviewing, thinking of that big picture, thinking of the implication to the masses and offering feedback along the way. Showering this team with your glitter and confetti and talking to those that continue to have doubts and frustrations with the process.

When this new thing is finally ready to roll out, you are the conveyor of the new. The teacher of the change. The one that makes this new thing the only thing people are using and talking about. You hype this thing up like only a spark can. Get yourself some balloons, some fire towers, some bangin' song and sell the heck out of it. Put on a show to end all shows and convince even the biggest doubter that this is going to be the best thing since the creation of the internet!

And then you monitor. You listen to the feedback. You tweak and you change as necessary and squash those naysayers and those that just won't get on board. You use that power of influence and sway until that is no longer needed.

And, because change is constant.... you just wash, rinse,

repeat. I promise you will be the biggest seller of change, even if you're not the one creating the entire process. And, quite honestly, that is just the way we like it!

Virtual Spark Applications:

- Be sure to include all the voices. In the virtual space, it is easy to forget certain groups or stakeholders. Be intentional with who you include in the change process and seek out new voices regularly.
- Allow space for commentary and questions. Since you won't see people in the halls of a physical building, create virtual drop-ins throughout the process to gather feedback and answer concerns.
- Have a plan for virtual share out at the start and end. Keep people in the know about the process through recordings and emails.

THE CUSTOMER IS ALWAYS RIGHT

HONESTLY, this is about the only thing that really matters. For. Real. Think about it. You could be living through the worst moment of your life, and when someone goes above and beyond to help, doesn't that make it slightly better? A kind word or act can change the trajectory of literally everything. As leaders we tend to quickly forget this ideal in our pursuit of greatness, but the simplest thing is really the biggest thing and one we can most quickly implement with literally no cost whatsoever.

A real-life example of this in action:

My husband and I recently visited a really small oyster bar near my childhood home. It seats about forty patrons. We rolled up at 8:15pm and got the last two seats at the bar. Upon entry we were greeted warmly by the entire staff, those in the kitchen, and behind the bar. When placing our order there were no expressions of frustration at our late arrival nor at our many questions about drinks or dishes. Food was served with a consistent smile.

About 9:00 pm the staff let everyone know that the kitchen was about to close. By this point, most of the customers had finished eating and were making their way out the door. My husband and I were finishing our most delicious whipped ricotta appetizer and had run out of the charred bread. We asked the bartender if we could get a few more pieces of bread, if any were available, and let them know we did not require the char, as we knew the kitchen was closed. The bartender could have very easily said there was no more bread. We would never have known. And yet, a few minutes later, a plateful of charred bread appeared, again with a smile. This small act of kindness and hospitality was not required, and yet the staff went above and beyond to meet our needs when they could have just as easily turned us down. This led to a very generous tip and the proclamation that our very first stop next time we are in town will be to the Delaware Avenue Oyster House.

And, because this is SO IMPORTANT, I am going to share a second story.

I am currently at a leadership retreat silently working on various parts of this book. The hotel in which I am writing is older and well, used, if you know what I mean. It would not, by any means, be my first choice of lodging in the city in which we are meeting. BUT I will say when I entered, I was given a bit of hope for wonderful possibilities by the fun and funky wallpaper behind the counter and the super creative business cards the manager was rocking.

Upon arrival in my room, I noticed several things:

1. The legs of the desk were rusty (definitely not new furniture)
2. The can surrounding the spotlight in the entry area was dusty (definitely not a new build)
3. The sticker on the mirror was from a different hotel brand.

Which led me to an early conclusion that this bleak and dreary location could not be saved by bright fun patterns and a cute title on a business card. Talk about going from the land of sunshiny hope and beautiful rainbows to a torrential downpour.

But that is when the importance and game-changing potential of excellent customer service comes in.

The staff at this hotel consistently went above and beyond with pleasantries, a can-do attitude, and suggestions for how to make our experience even better. Y'all. This made allllllllll the difference. I literally said, "I feel like a celebrity here. The staff is anticipating and catering to my every need," to a colleague.

Examples of some of the many ways in which I continued to feel the love and appreciation included the following:

1. A table was set up outside of our board room meeting space with a centerpiece and linens so that we could step out of the work zone and free our minds when needed.
2. When our snack was inadvertently forgotten, two employees brought drinks and a wide variety of options to us immediately upon request.
3. A variety of staff continuously checked on us at breakfast to ask about our coffee/juice needs and ensure everything was to our liking.
4. Continuous attention to our needs and requests throughout our time in the meeting room.

What at first appeared to be a negative situation quickly turned into a positive situation without any additional cost to the hotel. The rusty legs on my desk did not get fixed nor did the can in the ceiling. However, the things the staff could control, their attitudes and attention, were consistently high, thus ensuring we had the best experience possible, thus leading to the potential that we may one day return. If they had not been so accommodating and kind, we may have quickly and even possibly immediately begun to look elsewhere.

Remember this in all that you do. USE what is free and controllable when situations appear to be dire. Because it is only then that you can impact greater change.

All this adds up to the most important conclusion any leader can come to……the little things matter. BIG. In fact, they are probably the biggest difference maker in any organization, whether it be a 40-seat restaurant or an older hotel or a multinational corporation. Lee Cockerell, who is a former executive Vice President of Operations at Walt Disney World Resort said, "The soft stuff is actually the hard stuff but if you get it right, everything else tends to fall into place and turns out to be not so hard after all".

In the case of the Oyster Bar, it was definitely harder to take out the bread, slice it up (and dirty another utensil), fire up the grill and then serve it, then it was to just give us a few pieces, or most certainly far easier to tell us no, especially when that was what we were expecting. However, the staff took the time to do the hard stuff, thus giving them a returning customer and a bigger tip.

And in the case of the hotel, they certainly did not need to set us a table to free our minds or bring in extra snacks and drinks, or even smile as much as they did. However, their kindness and attention made us realize the important things in life and not be fixated on the things that don't matter, like rust and dust.

Let's think about how this applies to your organization… because it is applicable to all organizations. Are there times your employees have needs that you instinctively want to turn away? Is there someone that asks you for help at the very end of the day? Is there an employee who is going through a tough time who might need a little extra help with their responsibilities? What about a colleague that might need some guidance with a process or procedure that has been a standing policy or procedure for years? You may have to dirty some utensils and fire back up the grill when you thought you were done for the day to coax them through the situation. However, the sacrifice you make will repay you tenfold with their loyalty and their productivity once they get through their current obstacles.

This mentality is also contagious. When your employees receive this treatment, they want to "leave that big tip." And they do this by repaying the favor when someone comes to them in a similar situation. They begin to see the small stuff as the big stuff and how the little things can make the biggest impact.

Honestly, the little things are the easiest to control. You have direct control of your actions. You choose to do the little things, or you don't. This isn't always the case in the big things. Typically, in big impact situations there are multiple stakeholders included and lots of steps to reach the goal. Whereas in the little things, you can quickly implement change with very little thought. Because the little things truly go back to everything you learned in kindergarten….be kind to others. Treat them the way you want to be treated. Smile. Use your manners. Help where you can. Share. Make the bread. Take the call. These basic principles will never go out of style and will work again and again and again.

Virtual Spark Applications:

- This might be the hardest thing to gauge, since your staff is working remotely. You can check on them and their work, but you cannot see and hear what they are doing when you are not present. Have a process to gauge customer satisfaction. You can survey your stakeholders. You can meet with them on a regular basis. You can collect "complaints" and look for patterns. Although you can't "walk in on" customer/employee interactions as you can in the brick-and-mortar space, you can find ways to solicit feedback and use it to ensure expectations are being met.

- Set expectations and let staff know you will be checking to see these are met through customer satisfaction measures. Be clear about what good virtual service looks like. Give specific examples so there is a measuring stick for follow up conversations if needed.
- Model what you preach with your employees. If you expect them to answer communication with clients in 24 hours, do the same for them. If you expect emails to be free from grammar and spelling errors, be sure you do the same. Walk the virtual walk and talk the virtual talk in a way that translates to customer service.

PLAYING NICELY IN THE
SANDBOX

I MANAGED A VERY existential employee once. His spirituality was awe inspiring. Very Zen. Very calm. Very cosmic. It often took me quite a few minutes to fully understand where our conversations were heading and what exactly he needed. However, at the end of each session I was left feeling refreshed and fulfilled and hopeful, as was he. It was most certainly not my preferred style of communication. Nor was it my most utilized management style. But I learned very quickly that in order to get the highest performance out of him, I would need to adopt some of his ways. At least when communicating with him. And once I embraced that, I not only got a great performance from him, but I also got rewarded with some personal reflections that helped me to grow as a leader. The universe was definitely smiling down upon me!

Now had I treated this employee as I treated my many others, with succinct and direct communication, a detailed agenda of our time together, and quick responses, he probably would have floundered and most definitely would have ended up resigning. In order to maximize my influence on his performance, I had to bend into his "flow" and let go of some of my preferred methods. In short, I had to be more him and less me. Not that I changed the rules nor gave him extra grace. I just changed my leadership style slightly to better fit him. And the rewards were tremendous. You gotta give to get!

Fortunately, I have had many great role models in which to implement this management style of "more them, less me" concept. Because I am all sparkle and shine and fast and furious and my managers have, well, not had quite as much of that, yet they have been able to include the glitter when leading me, thus allowing me to reach my full potential. I have also had the unfortunate luck to have experienced the opposite, and much more common style. The firm. The constant. The detailed. The time sucker. The overly compli-cated. The impersonal. And, the very worst of all, the micro-manager.

I can say, in all honesty, when I am managed by someone who does not give in to my style, at least in some small way, my very first and strongest instinct is to retreat. To begin the search for something new. To figure out ways to avoid that person rather than to confide in that person. In fact, those that micromanage, question everything, ask for more details, want to meet all the time………. Well, their belief that control helps to grow makes me want to shrink and wither. And, I have seen first-hand that my personal hands-off approach has produced more who take on leadership roles than those that don't.

Now, of course, you must check behind people. AND when you see a situation that needs rectifying, you need to address and monitor. But I am not talking about employees with poor performance here. That is another situation that does require the firm and the detailed and the impersonal and the monitoring. No, I am talking about managing those that are performing well. That are self-sufficient producers. That can take on something new and important. Allowing them to make their own way, even when their way is different than your own, is imperative. Allowing them the space to stumble without fear and pick themselves back up gives them the confidence and the power to take the risks, try innovative options, and forge their own path without anyone unconsciously influencing them for their own gain. While leaders that love power might find this difficult, as they are fearful of negative outcomes, those that maintain a positive outlook and optimism will find it refreshing to let go and cheer from the sidelines. Coming in when needed and wanted.

And that part about bending to the person? Changing and adapting to their style? Well, here is where you let them take the lead. Listen while they talk and respond in a language they most appreciate. Is it academic? Simple? Flowery? Concise? Model and mimic their words to make them feel heard.

Do they want to meet All. The. Time? Need lots of reassurance? Or do they want to plow ahead and ask when guidance is needed?

And when in conversation do they need to vent? Share personal information? Ask questions? Get praise?

You will pick up much of this when you meet with them through natural conversation. But if you can't tell OR just want to jump right on in and get started ASK. Have them fill out a form about their needs. Or directly discuss in your next meeting. Determine THEIR style to ensure you are best able to serve.

While we all have our favorite style, one style does not fit all. Be sure to use the one that best fits as you meet with your people. Never change who you are and what you stand for, just change how you communicate and interact with those on your team. Sometimes you gotta go with the cosmic flow, and other times you gotta cut to the chase. Being chameleon-like in your approach will ensure your team is operating at top capacity and that you can celebrate with all the you-ness you got!

Virtual Spark Applications:

- Use feedback forms and surveys to determine employee needs and preferences. Then revisit it often to ensure you are playing nicely in the sandbox.
- Change meeting days/times/locations to ensure all needs are being met. If you need to meet once a week, consider alternating between morning and afternoon sessions or certain days of the week.
- Schedule times to talk about how collaboration is going and honestly hear the feedback. Make changes that serve the greater good.

CIRCLE UP YOUR
CHEERLEADERS!

As a leader, you are not going to have unlimited, unwavering support. Even if you are beloved. Even if you are the best leader that ever led. Because you must make SO MANY decisions continuously, your "popularity" will be fleeting and varied and, quite frankly, dependent on that day.

When I became the school leader, the term "lonely at the top" was never truer. I spoke to the same eight women on my leadership team daily, a few people above me frequently, and a collection of weekly contacts. But my daily interactions with the staff at large and the stakeholders in which they served dwindled to almost nothing. Yet the decisions I was making impacted them the most.

Despite many attempts at consistently connecting with my old gang of followers, time/space/leadership distance affected that connection and collaboration. And although I worked hard to consistently poll those in my charge and seek feedback and opinions often, the criticism and negativity would occur at various times, usually following changes that had the biggest impact. Although I KNEW this was natural and to be expected, it still stung, and, in the early days, shocked me after over a decade working with many now in my charge.

And that is where I relied heavily on my cheerleaders. Because it is SO EASY to get stuck in the muck. It is easy to believe the gloom and doom and begin to feel as if what you are doing is horrific and terrible and wrong. The women I was blessed to work with became my tribe. They would protect me from negativity as much as possible. They would defend me to the end. And they would help me find the humor and the good and the light when needed.

I will never forget the loyalty my team showed during a particularly tumultuous and toxic situation we were navigating together. We were facing a great deal of pushback from an outside group, who were trying to negatively control our narrative in all the backhanded ways. You know, manipulation, planting seeds of doubt, dividing and conquering. As the leader, I was always the first line of defense, working diligently to protect the team as much as possible from these toxins. However, they would seep through from time to time. And my team both saw the toll they were taking on me AND felt the toll themselves when I couldn't protect them. After months of this treatment, while together at a conference, the toxins were seeping through, affecting us all. A few of those who had been working against us were very vocal and obvious in a group setting about their intents. And to watch some of my quietest comrades explode with rage at the situation, along with my most vocal, made me realize their loyalty and support and all for one, one for all mentality was deep and strong and consistent.

And while having internal support is crucial, I also had to find external cheerleaders, because sometimes, those on the team may be the reason for stress and sadness and frustration. So having a strong tribe separate from the workspace to distract me from the sad days and the tough days is just as, if not more so, important. A group that can make me laugh at anything and everything but work. That listens objectively to difficult decisions I must and guide me through the journey. They will always save me when most needed. When I was having a literal nervous breakdown on a Saturday. When I don't think I can do this "one more day" and need them to help me remember my why. When I need to recharge my batteries with light and laughter and love, these cheerleaders are the only ones that can do it and will drop everything to do that when needed.

One of the last chapters is all about choosing to leave a place I loved. And my external tribe was there through alllll the ups and downs of that decision. Unlike my work tribe of the past, they still travel with me, now cheering me on in this newest chapter and helping me through all the tumultuous parts too.

And the King of my tribe. The one I COULD NOT do any of this without, is my super supportive spouse. Oh my goodness he is my biggest cheerleader! He believes 100000 percent that I can literally do anything. And he will shout it from the rooftops. He actually believes in me more than I believe in me, most days and is always there to listen, coach, guide, support, and encourage, no matter how big or crazy or scary my dreams may be.

This team is ready when needed.... morning, noon, or night. Weekends and holidays. 24/7 coming at me sideways. It isn't a large group, nor should it be. But it is a group that will literally pick me up off the floor, dry my tears, and encourage me to continue sparkling and shining through it all.

Find your tribe and love them hard. Celebrate them! Support them! Help THEM when they need it most. Cheer THEM on to greatness both in their professional and their personal lives. It is definitely give and take, even if it feels like you need them more than they need you. Go the extra mile with them, as they will go the extra mile with you. And be sure your thanks and your celebration come from the heart and are loud and proud and known to all. Because just as you need their loyalty, they need to see and feel and know you are just as loyal to them.

And no one can do it alone, so make sure those in your corner are those that will always be there, no matter the conditions, and will be there the entire season.

Virtual Spark Applications:

- Find your cheerleaders in unexpected places. They may not be on your direct team, so look for those connections in random situations, such as a one-off meeting or a face-to-face event. Once recognized, cultivate this relationship by asking for virtual time to collaborate and choosing this person to be on projects in which you need assistance.
- Think outside your virtual box! It is so easy to remain isolated in the virtual world. Look for connections outside of your organization and ask to connect to share ideas. LinkedIn is a great place to start, as are conferences and professional development sessions.
- Be sure your cheerleaders are well rounded. Virtual allows you to really pick and choose who you most communicate with. Evaluate your frequent emails, texts, and instant messages to determine if you are being cheered on by a homogeneous group or if there is a good variety of thoughts, ideas, and supports within the team.

THE DANGER ZONE CHAPTERS

DON'T LET YOUR SPARK BURN OUT OF CONTROL

THRIVING IN CHAOS

IT TAKES a certain level of madness to be a leader, doesn't it? I certainly think so. Your days are filled entirely with jumping from one challenging situation to the next, all while mixing in human emotions and unpredictability. You must be able to think on your feet, yet not get flustered. Be honest, but not TOO honest. Listen, yet tell. Show care and concern, but also tenacity and conviction. Basically, a constant contradiction of requirements. How else can you possibly describe leadership beyond simply thriving in chaos?

Leadership is messy. Unpredictable and varied. And the higher up I got, the more these things became true. At my highest level of leadership, I was asked by someone interviewing me, what a "typical day" in my life was like. I literally burst into laughter (thus perpetuating the leaders are mad theory). I have not had a typical day since 2013, when I became an Assistant Principal. I had a to-do list. I had a rough schedule. But more often than not, I was called into an unexpected situation. And thus, what I thought my day was going to look like, never materialized. In my early years, moving from teacher to administrator, my mind was

BLOWN by this non-stop chaotic schedule. And I was frustrated by the lack of progress on what I had HOPED to get done. But after realizing my job was less about tasks and more about people, I embraced the chaotic ways, and this has served me well.

I do believe my personality lends itself to this world. And certainly, my lifestyle. I am one who needs a lot of variety……. I mean, it is the spice of life, after all, isn't it? I often jump from one unfinished task to another. Folding laundry but oh wait, maybe I should go answer that email, but oh let me minimize that and order mom's birthday gift, but shoot, before I add to cart, let me run and check the mail, and then return to folding those shirts.

I also tend to want to go and go and go until I cannot go any more. Sure, it sounds fabulous to do the Aquarium Aglow at 5:30pm, followed by a nice dinner, and ending with a drive through the neighborhood to see the Holiday lights (this is literally the evening plan as I write this chapter). For most people one of those pursuits would be enough. But I want to cram it all in, jumping as quickly through all the things to keep my senses on high. Again, embracing all the chaos all the time.

And when it is quiet? And calm? Well, for me all is not bright and light. My mind runs. My heart races. What am I missing out on? What am I not doing that I should be? What could be accomplished during this idle time?? I have often found I do my best work when there are many things going on, as my energy level is high, and my mind is fully prepared for all things. It is warmed up and ready to go!

Now, don't get me wrong. There are times we NEED quiet. Rest is essential. And if you live at a speed of 100 miles per hour 24/7, 365, well, even the sparkiest of Sparks will burn out. And so, when I am away, I am AWAY. I tend to be one of those extreme people. (I cannot believe it has taken me fifty years to accept and acknowledge that.) But there is little middle ground. It is all or nothing all the time. I will give my all to the job and do all the things all the time at the highest level. But when I am taking the me time.........well, that is also getting my all....so full relaxation on the beach or a long run with music playing or savoring an exceptional meal with my loved ones and enjoying all the senses that entails.

YES, I thrive in chaos. But I know how to wrangle the chaos to keep things moving forward. Where to put the monkeys in the circus when the clowns are making people laugh and the acrobats are ready to fly. Know the power of keeping all things going, even when all things are divergent. And know the power of full separation when needed.

If you claim you like calm, organized, and well planned, this leadership thing might cause you to wither, because those words tend not to exist in the day-to-day operations of those in charge. Embrace the cray, welcome it in, and find ways to keep it as calm and organized as possible. And then, be sure you have built in your own calm and quiet at opportune times to make sure you don't run off with the circus, leaving the rest of the world behind!

Virtual Spark Applications:

- To say the virtual space is the epitome of chaos is an understatement. Things appear in various ways, needing your attention, thus getting pulled from one thing to another. Turn off notifications when in deep work, shut down all the tabs and focus on one, and set a timer to move from one thing to the next to ensure you can field all the tasks necessary.

- Block your calendar for important tasks and only focus on the task at hand during the time allotted. If you jump around, you will never finish what you started.
- Allow for flexibility when things arise and re-prioritize your day. Move things on your calendar to another day if needed and delete those "nice to dos."

WHEN TOO MUCH IS TOO MUCH

A FEW WEEKS AGO, I was driving my oldest to his first college visit (I know, I don't seem old enough to be taking a child to college ☺). It was dark and I was on an interstate highway I had never been on. The highway was under construction and most of the construction was being done at night. I may ACT young, but my eyesight is certainly NOT young, and neither is my energy level. Therefore, unfamiliar roads, in the dark, with lots of construction, had me on high alert.

What made things even worse, if possible, was the overload of signs and warnings about literally everything. Flashing signs. The standard yellow signs. Customized signs. Signs on the left. Signs on the right. Signs above. Signs. Signs. Everywhere were signs. Lane ends in 1 mile. Lane ends in .5 miles. Lane ends in .25 miles. Lane ends NOW. Left lane shifts. Do not pass on the left. Men at work. Left exit closed. Do not exit right. Exit 294 should exit on exit 291. Etc. Etc. Etc. It was the most overwhelming situation I may have ever driven through. It was literally impossible to understand all the directions or to know what was happening or where to go, so I attempted to stay in the center lane and thankfully did not need to exit at all through the construction zone. If I had, I am certain I would have either missed my exit or gotten off at the wrong one. And I am fully confident that Google Maps would never have been able to keep up with all the changes and modifications that were occurring.

I truly believe that the city and the construction workers placed all those signs there to help. They were trying to be proactive. To be clear. Because clear is kind. But.......... clear can sometimes be messy. Clear can sometimes be over-whelming. Clear can sometimes cause more confusion. AND it can cause MORE work for the people writing all the signs. Putting up all the directions. Creating all the lettering.

Leaders often spend lots of time and effort trying to be extremely clear. Preparing for every possible scenario. Spelling out every single direction. And in doing so, they take copious amounts of their own time creating these direc-tives, while causing their direct reports to have to read and attempt to follow their road signs. Some may greatly appre-ciate the down to the very last possible detailed road signs. But most get lost in the sheer number of signs, thus causing confusion along the way.

How do you find that balance between too little and too much? The Goldilocks, if you will....... not too cold, not too hot, but just right? Well, you need to solicit help from an outside source, a friend, spouse, relative, not in your world who can determine if what you are throwing out there makes sense but doesn't make things overly complicated.

I did that recently with my husband, and I held my breath when doing so. Because it is HARD to hear feedback when it is something you are proud of. And when it is something you poured your soul into? Well, it is scary to think that someone could rip it all apart. But you must be willing to take that chance to ensure it is excellent and makes sense and works. So, when creating my website for my business in a world in which I had limited knowledge and experience, I asked my husband to take a peek. While he quickly pointed out the great things, he also identified the too little and the too much. Namely, too much Edu speak that made things confusing for the average human. I thought I was sounding "smart," but what I was really doing was being confusing. He then passed my website along to a colleague, who said a lot more of the same. Together, the three of us worked through and found a path that was simple and easy to follow, while still getting my message across. Just the right amount of road signs to get the average person to the final destination easily. Not too hot and not too cold. Literally just right.

Stop making things more difficult on yourself. You cannot possibly think of every single possibility. I know this practice comes from a place of care and a place of preparedness. But it also brings a bunch of undue hardship on you and a bunch of unnecessary confusion on your team. Keep it simple, ask for feedback, and then roll it out with just the right amount of signage for maximum support. This allows everyone to get to the end of the journey in the most efficient way possible, yourself included.

Virtual Spark Applications:

- Virtual space allows for virtual vastness. Meaning, you can spend countless hours trying to perfect all the details. You don't usually have to react immediately to problems, as the problems may take time finding their way to you. But just because you have the time doesn't mean you need to use the time. Treat all situations as you would in the real world. If the response only requires a sentence, don't write a novel. If the explanation can be done in 3 minutes, don't stretch it to 30.

- Remember that being too detailed in the process can lead to confusion and rigidity. While virtual communication allows for clear direction, making things so finite can leave remote employees uncertain, even after the best intentions. Keep it simple, stupid and schedule a Q&A session if you think copious amounts of finite details will be needed.

- Remember that time is your most important commodity. And perfection is impossible. Use your time wisely and don't waste it seeking to make that document/presentation/email/recording flawless. It is an impossible endeavor and one that will hurt you in the long run by wasting your energies on a fruitless pursuit.

WHOOPSIE!

As SOMEONE who likes to jump first and look later, I have made my fair share of mistakes. And while in my "old age" I have become slightly better at thinking before acting, I am still a risk taker at heart. I do believe with great risk comes great rewards, but I also know with great risk can come great catastrophe…. definitely a crap shoot sometimes. However, you don't know until you try, and I am a big believer in trying until you get it right.

But what, as a leader, do you do when your risks turn into dumpster fires? When you jump confidently but land badly? How do you handle the mistakes you will inevitably make because you are not only human, but also because you are brave?

Well, easy. You are honest. You are transparent. You are human. AND you do these things BEFORE the jumping or the risks.

You present your grand (or not so grand) idea to the masses, and you give these caveats……….

" This could be a dumpster fire however, I believe it could also lead us to the land of sunshine and rainbows,".

And

"We are about to jump in hopes we find gold, but know if we don't, we could land amongst the thorns,".

USE YOUR SPARKINESS TO THE MAXIMUM. Sell that idea but don't paint such a glorious picture that failure seems impossible. Put the risk out there loud and proud. And own the responsibility for the fall. Even if some of it is not your doing. Even if someone else forgot to pack the chutes. You are the one bringing the risk, so you are responsible for every bump that comes along.

When things get a little off track during the journey, don't just own the misstep publicly, find ways to apologize in smaller doses. Personally and immediately. Every action has consequences. And when the consequences cause strife or hardships, be sure to be there to help make those go away. You cannot fully understand the depth of the mistake in a large group setting. Only by having those intimate discussions can you problem solve the problem you created and work together on a plan for improvement. And then, your big, grand idea will come to fruition.

But what about those smaller mistakes? Those that aren't part of risk or bravery or outside of the box thinking? What about those mistakes that are just, well, mistakes? Those that you cannot be prepared for. That just happened. Maybe you said the wrong thing in a meeting. Maybe you promised something you can't deliver. Maybe you gave inaccurate information. While it might seem small to you, it can have a big and lasting impact on others. The rule of apologizing always applies in all situations.

There are times a whole group apology may work. If you promised something you could not deliver to many, the best route would be to publicly acknowledge that error. But usually, quick and unintended mistakes occur in much smaller pockets. Usually in one on one or small group settings. If the mistake is made in such a way, be sure to apologize to the same group. AND always, always, always, always do so face to face. NEVER do so in writing. Not only does this seem impersonal, but it also allows for misinterpretation. Be your brave, bold self and own all your actions.

Bottom line, you are probably going to be harder on yourself than others when you fumble. Particularly if you act with honesty and integrity and transparency. Expect things to falter. And be prepared as much as possible when they do. Know that you are making more of your mistakes than others, but still allow those affected by your errors the time to express their frustrations. And then pick yourself up and forge on like only you can! Without mistakes, we would have no growth. As Albert Einstein once said, "Anyone who has never made a mistake has never tried anything new,", and he turned out pretty ok, so I know you will too!

Virtual Spark Applications:

- Own the big mistakes in a big way. Don't just send an email admitting fault, call staff together to own it and discuss ways you will improve in the future.
- Apologize to those most affected individually. Grab them for a quick virtual call. Send them a handwritten note. Ask them for feedback on how you can improve the next time.
- Don't forget to reflect on these setbacks to ensure they do not happen again. Keep a
- "I could do better" Google Doc or Note on your phone and add to it when things occur. Review it regularly to avoid making the same mistake twice.

A SPOONFUL OF SUGAR MAKES
THE MEDICINE GO DOWN

HERE'S the thing about difficult conversations. Even the toughest person, with the strongest conviction in the need for the difficult conversation to be had, absolutely hates and dreads those conversations. As humans, we do not seek out conflict. We are wired to avoid danger at all costs. And conversations that may lead to anger or sadness or frustration or negativity are dangerous. We fear hurt feelings. We fear lash outs. We fear tears. We also fear messing them up and making things worse. Anyone with even the slightest bit of empathy does not wake up in the morning hoping to make someone feel bad.

Let's take that out of the equation.... the feelings you feel when you know you must have a difficult conversation, because we all have them. Instead, let's focus on what you can control, that is factual and tangible. Because, you know, you cannot control how anyone feels, including yourself, so coaching you through feelings is pointless.

Whenever I must do something difficult and something I hate, I always rely on the following best practices to make that difficult thing less bearable.

1. **Working to get it done as quickly as possible**. I HATE when things linger. It makes those things seem so much bigger. Plus putting off the inevitable does not make it go away. Therefore, if you know you must have a difficult conversation find time to have that conversation as soon as possible.
2. Prior to the conversation, **gather all facts and pertinent information.** Never go into a situation unprepared. Have talking points ready. Have facts and statistics if necessary. Be sure you are not scrambling to gather what you need in the moment.
3. **Rehearse your words**. If you don't have a trusted friend or colleague to bounce ideas off, then do it in the mirror or at your desk or while driving.
4. **Expect reactions and be prepared with responses.** Think of possible answers/rationale to what you are saying and how you will respond. You cannot possibly be prepared for every reaction, but you can probably guess a few based on the person and the situation, so have your answers ready.

Knowing that I am as ready as possible makes walking into that conversation slightly easier.

Once there, I utilized the following to get through the situation as efficiently and productively as possible.

1. Start with very short (and I mean like 30 seconds or less) pleasantries. We all know why we are in the meeting, but starting with a positive never hurts. Ever.

2. Present a brief reasoning for the conversation. Give facts and examples. Leave out emotions as much as possible (and boy is this hard for a Spark!)
3. Allow time for the other person to speak. Do not interrupt, even when you feel they are presenting inaccurate information. Allow them the full time to give their side and opinion. Take notes, if necessary, while they are talking and let them know you are doing so to help better understand.
4. Summarize what you heard and ask if your understanding is accurate. This is super important for later. You must be clear in what you are addressing and certain the other party understands this as well.
5. Despite the feelings presented by the other party, work to keep your emotions neutral. Stick to facts as much as possible.
6. If the conversation is going nowhere, or getting too heated for productivity, take a break. Not for a long period, but allow for 30 minutes or so to calm down and gather thoughts and then jump back in.
7. Work to agree on mutual outcomes. If this is disciplinary, be sure to have this set-in advance, along with consequences if the outcomes are not met.
8. Set a time to follow up on the discussion to gauge effectiveness of the outcome and determine if more conversation is needed.

Like every single thing that happens in life, practice makes perfect. You may fumble a few of these items the first few times you utilize them. You may forget to do something either in advance or in the moment. And that is fine because my last tip is the most crucial and that is:

Be human. Be honest. Be vulnerable.

Admit mistakes. Apologize when necessary. Sympathize and seek to understand. Show your human side and your relatability as these will make those on the receiving end of a challenging talk much more willing to accept whatever it is you are giving out. Be kind but firm. Be clear and concise. Treat the person like you would like to be treated when receiving challenging news. If you can do that, you will have a far greater chance at success, so lean into this above all else and rely on the above as your most important tool.

And then, CeLeBrAtE the talk being done. Even if not finalized or finished or complete. Breathe that sigh of relief. Go grab an extra cup of coffee. Eat that Hershey's Kiss. Because doing hard things requires doing good things for yourself. Do it and then give yourself permission to do better next time and celebrate bigger too. Getting through with a happy light at the end makes anything seem possible.

Virtual Spark Applications:

- Do. This. LIVE! Never, ever, ever, ever, ever, ever attempt to have a difficult conversation through email. Ever. Find time to meet virtually, with cameras on, and discuss the situation together.
- Do not let things linger. Find time to meet ASAP. Even if it requires moving meetings and tasks. That is the beauty of virtual flexibility–the opportunity to make changes quickly to schedules and tasks.
- Take notes while talking. OR if you feel the conversation needs to be revisited, record it. And be sure to let the other party know you are doing so, to be fully transparent.

ARE THEY HAPPY ABOUT
ANYTHING?

I AM certain you have come across a Negative Nelly/Ned/Nemesis in your time as a leader. You know the type. The staff member who will complain about literally everything. And not just those things that are workplace related or even relevant. In fact, more often than not, the complaints are things well outside of the scope of control and are usually so insignificant it leaves a leader wanting to spend vast amounts of time and energy complaining about THEM.

Here are a few examples, in case you have been so blessed as to live in the positivity bubble that you don't have experience with the Negative Ns of the world.......

ME: Good morning! **Negative N:** Not really! I overslept, stubbed my toe, got stuck in traffic, spilled my coffee, and then opened the meanest email ever.

Me: I brought everyone coffee today! **Negative N**: It is not the right temperature and I don't like to drink from paper cups.

Me: Here is a $50 gift card to thank you for persevering during this rough week! **Negative N**: Oh, so we are being thanked for just doing our jobs AND with plastic that is killing the environment?!?

YOU GET MY DRIFT………. those people that can NEVER find the light, even when it is literally blinding them.

One of my all-time favorite complaints came anonymously when asking for feedback following a staff meeting. We stupidly asked for feedback on the breakfast food provided and one of the comments was written in all caps "DONUTS ARE NOT BREAKFAST!" :) I mean our fault for asking for opinions. However, it was a free donut and one we were not obligated to provide, yet that person felt the need to vehemently express their thoughts. That situation was literally over a decade ago and yet it still comes to the forefront of my mind when thinking of complainers.

And I'll be honest, I have spent way too much time trying to "fix" those kinds of complaints. Because I feel like the donuts, coffee, gift card complaints are somewhat in my sphere of control. Ok, so next time we will serve pastries, have a coffee bar, and give cash. Next time, we will not have one single complaint. Next time we will make EVERYONE happy.

But here is what I learned. You can't do that. Ever. No matter what. Even if you have donuts and egg whites and fruit and caviar and salmon and bagels…. someone is going to want bacon. Even if you bring the team to a coffee shop and tell them to order whatever they want on the menu. Someone is going to want a different coffee shop. Even if you give a $5000 thank you. Someone is going to say you should have donated to charity/put it in their salary/given more.

I am not sure why this is. I have also spent way too much

time trying to figure out the why, both for specific individuals and for society at large. And that rabbit hole is just as dangerous to go into as the "try to make everyone happy" hole.

Instead, I shift MY thinking when I encounter the Negative Ns. I remember to embrace who I am and celebrate my joy and stop trying to make others feel the same. I also tend to avoid those Negative Ns as much as possible. At meetings I will give cursory hellos and goodbyes, with all the usual sparkness, but I won't dilly dally or attempt to try to combat their negative with my positive. Nope. No more!

I have also learned to only ask about the things that really matter and are crucial to an organization's success. If you want to bring in coffee, GREAT, and if someone doesn't want it, GREAT. No need to ask why. No more polls about breakfast foods or thoughts on the chosen hotel. I used to think that showed CARE to ask for opinions on trivial matters. But it only shows care if the individual's opinions and feelings are satisfied. And with a staff of over 200, it was impossible to satisfy all feelings. So, instead of surveys following events, we listened during the events to comments such as:

I wish you had gluten free donuts so I could enjoy one.

I would love a way to reshare my $50 with someone who needs it more.

Since I can't have caffeine, I will pass on coffee today.

These unsolicited statements have been found to be much more important than random complaints. They have an unbiased and factual base. And they are constructive as opposed to destructive and allowed us the ability to do better next time.

Bottom Line: Always follow your heart. Always spread joy, even to those who appear to be joyless. Stop trying to understand their reasoning and rather listen closer to those who have a reason to give feedback and lean in there. That, my friends, will bring YOU greater joy than anything else, and will help quiet those Negative Ns in the hopes that their voices will quiet and disappear into their own sad, spark-less minds.

Virtual Spark Applications:

- It is easy to avoid Negative Ns in the virtual space. Do not seek them out if you know they will only bring you down. Obviously work with them when needed, but certainly don't make them a priority for general banter and opinions on non-crucial items.
- If they share negativity in the written form, and it is continuously egregious, collect the evidence, then share it with them in a nonthreatening manner. They may not realize how their tone is being perceived in the virtual space.
- Pick and choose your battles. If the employee is just a sourpuss in virtual meetings but highly effective in productivity, you may want to ignore the behaviors. However, if you sense they are leading the negativity bus and causing others to follow, addressing the behavior with norms and expectations for virtual meetings should help quell the behavior.

SKATERS

Y'ALL. My son is a skater. And not the kind on a skateboard. Or ice. Nope. Both of those take passion and conviction and grit. No, my son is a skater who literally just wants to skate on through life, effortlessly. He doesn't necessarily want to LEARN to do the things, he just wants to get on his skates and slide on by, without fighting to get there or trying to learn tricks and stunts to make his skating stand out.

And what is THE MOST FRUSTRATING THING as his mother is that this boy is brilliant. I mean, ridiculously so. And I knew it from an early age. He knew his ABCs and 123s by sight at 18 months. He was pointing out the capitals of various third world countries at age four. And he was a Junior Scholar by Middle School, scoring in the top 5% of all Middle School Students in the state of South Carolina on the PSAT without any preparation or practice.

However, he has never, not one time, even slightly applied his big old brain to be the best of the best. He never won the spelling bee. He never placed in the Math League. He wasn't the top graduate in his class or even qualified for the National Honor Society at his High School. And as a mother, knowing he COULD do all these things and more if he just put in the teeniest bit of effort drives me batty.

Our daily conversations go something like this...

ME: Hey Buddy. I just saw this amazing opportunity. I think you should investigate it. It is about XYZ which you love.

The Son: Ok. Sounds good.

Me: What did you do about that other amazing opportunity I shared with you yesterday?

The Son: Oh, I forgot.

Me: Did you not think it looked amazing?

The Son: I did.

Me: So why didn't you investigate it?

The Son: (shrugs shoulders)

Me: I just don't understand, Buddy. Not sure what motivates you. You say you love XYZ but when there is an opportunity to explore and advance with XYZ you don't do anything about it. It worries me tremendously.

The Son: I know Mom. I know. I will look into it now.........

Wash. Rinse. Repeat. For 16 years.

BUT HERE'S THE THING. He is doing REALLY WELL at what he is expected to do as a 16-year-old. He is getting all As and Bs at the best High School in the state. He is involved in several extra-curricular activities, and all the adults leading those activities constantly comment on what a kind and encouraging young man he is. He is helpful around the house and always compliant and agreeable. In fact, as I write this, I realize he is pretty much the perfect kid!

He may be skating by in my eyes. But in the eyes of the

world, he is far exceeding expectations. And that is all that should really matter.

Let's apply this example to the workspace.

At this very moment, I am knee deep in end of year reviews. And while completing those for the highflyers is fun and those for the employees that seriously suck are easy, the ones that do the bare minimum requirements? Those that do just enough but not a teensy bit more? Those that skate on by? THOSE are the hardest.

Because if you are reading this book, you are one that strives to be better. To do more. To grow. To shine. To achieve. It probably irks you to no end when someone is not those things.

BUT here is the thing, if someone is doing exactly what you have asked, how can you fault them? If they are doing the requirements of their job, how can you lay blame?

You see, we need people to work. We need people to get the job done. And, if I am being honest, you WANT people to show up, get it done, and go back home. Because...you cannot have an organization full of leaders. You cannot have a whole crew of people who want to spend time making changes and sharing ideas. Unless you work in an organization of single digits, having a group of go-getters with all the passion for all the things will cause you to spend copious amounts of time listening, guiding, answering questions, discussing, and explaining and that will wear you out real quick like.

You may argue, I want SOME passion from the people. A few opinions. A few thoughts. Some sign of love for what they do. You ever heard that expression, you can't have it all? Well, insert that here.

The problem with skaters may just be YOU. You set expectations but then want people to exceed them. You want opinions and thoughts, but not all the thoughts and opinions. You know what you DON'T want but you can't quite articulate exactly what you do. How to fix this quandary?

Well, first start with your minimum expectations. Are they set too low? Do you need to revisit with your leadership team and share out amongst the masses? With organizational growth comes the need for organizational change. Be sure to set time to do this often.

If you find your expectations are on course, and you still have a handful of skaters, your next step would be direct conversations with those employees. Find out what motivates them and encourage them to step into areas in which they can shine. See if you can give them a small push to do a little more. You may discover hidden talents and ideas that could better serve your organization.

If that push doesn't work, you may need to have a very direct conversation with the employees at hand as to their future with your organization. What is motivating them to stay when it appears their heart is not in it? This may be risky, as this very conversation may cause them to rethink and find other pastures, but at the end of the day, wouldn't you rather have someone dedicated to your cause than those that just are? That is the question YOU must weigh. How much skating is too much and when it is time to ask people to skate on? The one advantage of this risk is that this final push may just push those skaters over the line into the world of higher achievers. And if that risk is worth that reward, I say take it.

"There is a lot of stuff we can't control, but it is completely in our power to decide what the definition of a good job is. That's up to us." - Mike Rowe

And if an employee's definition of a good job and your definition of a good job are mismatched, losing them might not be such a bad thing after all.

. . .

Virtual Spark Applications:

- Skaters can skate free and far and frequently in the virtual world unless there are clear measures to hold them to as it is so easy to hide behind the keyboard. Set frequent benchmark checks that can be as simple as a weekly conversation, a checklist that is shared and marked off when tasks get done, or a due date with a presentation by the employee of tasks completed. And then find the areas in which the skater is shining and give them more of that.
- Look for those that are not skating and loudly and proudly celebrate them. Then conference with your skating crew and use the non-skaters as examples for which someone can strive. Help them set goals with benchmarks such as those above and encourage them to rise to the occasion through email cheer and motivational texts.
- Review the virtual norms you have set. If they are too slack, tighten them up, share them out, and then begin to hold staff to the new expectations.

THERE IS NO I IN TEAM

IF I HAVE LEARNED nothing more in my time as a leader, it is this–if you lead at least one person, you better be sure to expect some dysfunction and conflict. Even the strongest and most cohesive teams face disagreements from time to time, so having the tools to work through these situations will be crucial to sustained team success.

How can you be prepared for the inevitable? Here are some tried and true tips:

First and foremost, you must figure out the root cause of the conflict. Because it may present itself as one thing, but really be oh so much deeper. For some groups, it is the inability to make a key decision and nothing more. For others it may be a team member not pulling their weight, causing feelings of resentment. Or it may be all out dislike and disdain for those on the team.

Now, your first instinct might be to get the team together and directly address the problem. But this almost never works. Because…. there are feelings. There are emotions. There is passion. And bringing all that together in a time of turmoil almost guarantees a fire.

Instead, have one on one conversations with each team member to get their insights. This allows for several things to occur. First, it allows the staff members to vent. To be heard. To be able to present their thoughts and opinions in their entirety without distraction or interruption. This is NOT the time to interject your own thoughts or opinions. It is simply a time to listen. Doing so will allow you to understand if the issue is really the only issue, or if there are other events that are contributing to the situation that will need to be addressed. It also allows for time to heal some wounds. The closer you are to the disastrous situation, the worse it is. Time allows for all to reflect and simmer, to better come to an agreement.

Following those conversations, set up a meeting with the entire team and be sure to let them know the goal is to resolve the issue so that it ceases to be a cause of conflict. Come to that meeting with a plan and action steps. Do not go into it serving as a neutral third party. Be ready to provide clear guidance and expectations for the team dynamics in the future.

Once in the meeting, remind the group that this is not the time to air the grievances. The grievances have already been heard, thanks to your one on ones. Allow someone to start with their thoughts, feelings, and emotions, but redirect if anything should become accusatory, disrespectful, or unproductive. Once everyone has said what they feel needs to be shared, ask for solutions. Allow for gives and takes throughout the process. Diffuse hostility as needed. Allow for a break or regroup if it seems as if the team is not ready to work towards the solution.

At the end of this, a plan must be made to move forward. And that plan might very well be to figure out how to restructure teams in the future. Maybe department changes are needed. Maybe roles need to be shifted. And if that is the case, you should let the team know you are going to find a way to "maximize everyone's skills so they can thrive". This gives them light at the end of the tunnel to know their current situation isn't forever.

But if things can be amicably resolved, your work is not done. Check in with this team frequently and often to ensure they are not back sliding. Make sure they know to come to you before a situation, such as the most recent controversy, occurs again. And give them the tools to handle conflict appropriately in the future, such as books, articles, or talking points.

Again, every team will face conflict. But being as proactive and as prepared as possible will allow those involved to work through and continue to cohesively tackle all in which they are charged.

Virtual Spark Applications:

- Schedule one on ones with each person back-to-back. Don't leave too much time between meetings, so that all information is gathered and absorbed around the same time. Take notes while stories are shared.
- Allow time to formulate a plan to move forward. You do not need to act immediately. Give wait time to all involved and schedule something for a few days after the share-out at a time in which the parties are most likely to be actively engaged and focused (i.e., not a Friday afternoon. Not first thing in the morning. Not right after lunch).
- Follow up virtually consistently. Set individual and group check-ins and give plenty of notice so that

no one is blindsided and feels the opportunity to give the new process a chance, while also knowing there will be further chance for change.

DELIVERY IS EVERYTHING

I ALWAYS LOVED those choose your own adventure books growing up. You know the ones where you are given a scenario and then you must pick between two options as to how you would handle it? The scenario is constant, but the outcomes are vastly different based on your choices.

I'm about to give you the opportunity to have a similar experience with a real-life leadership choice. You will have two options following a review of the below scenario. Be sure to choose wisely, as the fate of this employee hangs in the balance!

SCENARIO: You manage an employee in a very high-level leadership role. This employee has years of leadership experience but is new to this role. She has longevity in the organization and great success in all previous roles. However, this position is vastly different from all others, as she now oversees several different departments, in which she has limited experience and expertise. She also transitioned from being peers with the leaders of those various departments to being their manager.

Despite this great learning curve, she had some pretty big successes in re-structuring the leadership team, helping make necessary changes to departments in need, maintaining a high level of job satisfaction by the staff, and onboarding a brand-new to the organization team member to the leadership team for the first time in the organization's history. There were challenges and learning curves in the communication and implementation of these changes, and certainly opportunities for growth. However, from a big picture perspective, she met the minimum requirements of the role consistently.

From a personal perspective, this employee has been open and transparent with her direct manager, throughout the year, as to her thoughts around if this was the role for her. The stresses on her took a toll, both mentally and physically and impacted her work life balance considerably. However, that never stopped her from giving her 100% to the position and all that was required, and she certainly never shared this with her direct reports or the organization. Rather, she used her manager as a sounding board and a confidant.

As her manager, you now have 90 minutes to talk to her about her performance after one year in the role. Which of the following approaches would you take?

○ **OPTION ONE:** Focus on her areas of improvement and make those details the primary emphasis for your discussion, minimizing successes for the sake of ensuring she understands the need to make changes. If this is your choice, please go to option one to see how the story continues.

○ **OPTION TWO**: Celebrate her wins and accomplishments, recognizing her feelings were valid and natural and use her readily identified growth areas as an opportunity to demonstrate how she can learn and grow. If this is your choice, go to the second option to see how the story continues.

OPTION ONE:

Manager: Before we start the review, I would like to hear your thoughts on how you think you did this year.

Leader: Well, as you know, it's been challenging. There were times I felt like I was not going to make it. However, it is not in my nature to just give up. Nor would I ever leave this organization in the lurch as I am passionate about serving the staff. I am also extremely proud of all that we have accomplished here. I'm really pleased by the fact that I did not give up despite these difficulties and that I learned how to handle challenging situations. I am hopeful that this next year will not be quite as difficult due to my knowledge and practice in the role. Furthermore, some of the big changes I have made this year are allowing me to see the light at the end of the tunnel and believe that these changes are going to be the difference maker not only for the organization but for me personally. I am confident in these new directions, and I am certain that they will help drive great success. For the first time since I have been in this role, I am excited to come to work every day and hopeful for the future. I will take that as a win.

Manager: Well, that's great. I know you have been very doubtful about this job all year. Now let's jump into your review. First, let's talk about data. Your team set lofty goals that you did not meet. Furthermore, the goals were not aligned which could've made it difficult for you to keep up with and monitor. I wish you had thought that through when setting the goals because it seemed like all you did was scramble. Is that accurate?

Leader: Well, yes and no. I mean, it would have been great to have everyone doing the exact same thing, but that is difficult in our environment. And I wouldn't say I scrambled. I did juggle a lot and had to learn a lot, but I think that came more from my lack of experience in the role than it did with the diverse goals.

Manager: Hmmm. Ok. Then why do you think the goals were not attained?

Leader: I aimed too high, and I now see how that is causing stress amongst the team, since we didn't meet our goals.

Manager: So, it sounds like you blame yourself for the failures?

Leader: I mean, ultimately it is my responsibility to ensure goals are met. But I would say we didn't fail. We just didn't meet our very ambitious goals.

Manager: Let's move to talking about your ability to thrive in this role. You have said numerous times you don't feel this is the job for you. Do you think that hindered your ability to be highly effective?

Leader: I really don't. Although I personally do not feel fulfilled by it, and miss connecting with others, I know I consistently gave 110% and made some significant impacts.

Manager: You mention connecting with others. I feel you are doing too much with your team. As the leader, you should start to separate, and I don't think you have done a good job doing that. You want them to know you are in charge and to respect boundaries. They are no longer your colleagues, but rather your subordinates.

Leader: Yes, I understand that. As do they. I have never felt taken advantage of by them OR afraid to let them know when they need to make changes. We have a built-in layer of trust and respect that allows us to be a true team.

Manager: Well, I stand by this, and I am hopeful it doesn't lead to your downfall. Finally, let's talk about your ability to market and promote the organization. I feel you have not been political enough nor strategic enough, would you agree?

Leader: Well, I am not a politician, so yes, I would agree I am not political. But strategic? I think I made necessary organizational changes that allowed us to begin to take the steps needed to reach those lofty goals. But I will never put "political" decisions over relationships and culture. I believe I have found a way to do what is needed without politicking and that is through open, honest communication and transparency.

Manager: After much review, I have deemed you as having an effective year, although there are great areas for improvement and without those changes discussed today, I am not sure how much longer you will be able to be successful in this role.

How does this story end?

It ends with the Leader doubting everything about themselves. It ends with the Leader wanting to quit right then and there. It ends with tears. By the end of the week, the Leader has updated her resume and has spent hours searching for other options and rethinking everything about her choices both from the year as the leader and her career. She will continue, but with doubts and fears around her ability to thrive and succeed.

Option Two:

121

Manager: Before we start the review, I would like to hear your thoughts on how you think you did this year

Leader: Well, as you know, it's been challenging. There were times I felt like I was not going to make it. However, it is not in my nature to just give up. Nor would I ever leave this organization in the lurch as I am passionate about serving the staff. I am also extremely proud of all that we have accomplished here. I'm really pleased by the fact that I did not give up despite these difficulties and that I learned how to handle challenging situations. I am hopeful that this next year will not be quite as difficult due to my knowledge and practice in the role. Furthermore, some of the big changes I have made this year are allowing me to see the light at the end of the tunnel and believe that these changes are going to be the difference maker not only for the organization but for me personally. I am confident in these new directions, and I am certain that they will help drive great success. For the first time since I have been in this role, I am excited to come to work every day and hopeful for the future. I will take that as a win.

Manager: Well, that's great. I know you have been very doubtful about this job all year, but you have done some amazing things for it being your first year in the role. AND you have identified growth areas that I know you will begin immediately improving. I cannot wait to see where you go from here. It can only get better!

Now let's jump into your review. First, let's talk about data. Your team set lofty goals! I was impressed by your ambition. I know everyone was disappointed when they were not met, though, so talk to me about how you plan to balance that next year.

Leader: While I am a big thinker and dreamer, I have learned the importance of baby steps and realism! Sure, we want to slay our goals, but having a gradual plan to get to them is key, and something I am working on with the team as we speak.

Manager: Wonderful! I figured you would have a plan to combat that. Please include me in these conversations and let me know how I can help.

Now, let's move to talking about your ability to thrive in this role. You have said numerous times you don't feel this is the role for you. Have you had a change of heart, now that you have a year under your belt? Is there anything I can do to better support you during the upcoming year?

Leader: I am still not 100% certain this is the best fit for me, BUT I am pleased with where we are ending the year, given the challenges faced. You know I am always going to give my all and never give up, so I plan to do just that and see how things are progressing this coming year. Change is certainly hard, and I am hopeful with some practice and familiarity under my belt, this year will be even better for us all.

Manager: Great reflection! Yes, the first year is almost always impossible to feel great comfort and success. As mentioned, I think you have done an outstanding job given this fact.

Now, let's talk about your sweet spot, connecting with others. I know this comes naturally to you and the area in which you most shine. Do you ever feel like your ability to connect can hinder progress at times?

Leader: I could see how it could at times. But I have worked alongside this team for over a decade. There are natural connections and friendships that won't and shouldn't just end. I am not afraid to hold anyone accountable, but I know I must set aside historical feelings at times and that may delay necessary change at times. It isn't easy and something I struggle with daily.

Manager: Totally natural and understandable! I would

advise when you are doubting the actions of your team or wondering if you are giving too much grace based on the relationships, to find someone to bounce the situation off. Doesn't have to be me but I am always happy to lend an ear.

Finally, let's talk about how this role is so different from previous ones you have held and how you think you have modified practices to rise to the needs of the job. Do you feel you have what it takes to lead in a way different from your previous responsibilities?

Leader: I have struggled with this as well. I went into this role thinking it was just a souped-up version of my previous role, which has always been the case with my leadership trajectory. But I have quickly learned this role requires a lot more external relationship building than the internal ones. And I have had to mourn this, because you know I love my people. But I am learning to love new friends and working to build those external relationships to ensure our organization continues to thrive and grow.

Manager: Wonderful! I knew you would be able to manage that given your proven history of relationship building. After much review, I have deemed you as having an effective year. You have done a great job in fostering both new and old relationships and driving urgency around goals, but you know you still have room to grow in both areas. You also acknowledge and recognize your areas for improvement, and I am certain you will continue to make great strides in that area. I also know you have and continue to doubt your ability to do this. I KNOW you can have great success in this role given time and reflection BUT I also know you must WANT to be in this role, given the stress and scope of the job, so take some time to reflect on this and know I am always here to be a thought partner.

· · ·

How does this story end?

It ends with the Leader recognizing growth areas while being confident that she has what it takes to meet her goals. She is valued for the good things she did, yet understands she has improvements to make. She enters her second year with actionable growth areas and support from her manager, leaving her feeling hopeful and confident.

Giving feedback is the most powerful tool you have as a leader. It allows you the opportunity to ensure your mission and vision is being carried out in the way you see fit. However, messaging and knowing who you are delivering your message to and how they best receive that message is crucial. Your time one-on-one with your employees is the most important way to drive change in your organization. It is crucial that if you do nothing else you do this well.

There are most certainly some employees that benefit and need a focus on growth areas, and there are also some employees that benefit and need a focus on their wins. And these foci can change throughout the course of an employee's lifetime with your organization. And by that, I mean, there may be times you will have to lean on one more than the other, and then revert during the next conversation. Because human beings are not static. They are constantly evolving and changing and shifting in their thoughts and their actions and their feelings. As leaders, we must be aware of how to best deliver such crucial and career changing information. It is truly the most important responsibility a leader has.

Virtual Spark Applications:

- Despite distance, you know when someone is upset during a conference. Allow for pauses and starts and stops if necessary.

- If you feel a conversation did not go as planned, follow up with reasons why in writing. Both to put closure on the situation and to ensure your voice is heard.
- Don't only focus on negative data/situations. It is easy to fall into this virtual trap, since time with staff is limited and data is so readily available. Be sure to always look for the positive and highlight it through difficult conversations.

THE SIMMERING CHAPTERS

*WHEN IT IS TIME TO LET YOUR SPARK
BURN OUT*

IT'S SO HARD TO SAY GOODBYE

SOMETIMES IT IS easy to make the decision to let people go. Those that are underperforming and/or not performing or directly violating policies and procedures are no brainers. Still not the most pleasant of conversations and not one anyone relishes, but not one that is tough to decide.

But what about those hard-working, been around a long time, top performers? What if they are starting to lose sight of the vision and mission? What if they are stale and stagnant? What if they are downright bitter and frustrated and do nothing to sustain the culture and productivity, yet do the bare bones of their jobs? How do you say goodbye to someone who really isn't doing anything terribly wrong from a performance perspective and has put in their time with your organization and, at one time, been a top performer?

It is not easy, that is for sure.

Because ...

You may understand the reason they are jaded. You may sympathize with their frustrations. And you may agree with some of their negative sentiments. If you have been anywhere long enough, you will have experienced disappointments and letdowns by those in charge.

But feeling those feelings in small pockets for small moments is certainly vastly different from living and breathing them out into the organizational culture minute after minute, hour after hour, day after day.

How do you address something that isn't typically evaluated (but should be)? How do you help someone either get back on or jump off when it appears they have no desire to do either? How do you help someone see that what they think is where they need to be, really is not?

Well, you start with your best attribute…. that emotional reaction. You listen and sympathize. You observe and comment. You help that employee to see what others so easily see, that it might be time to say goodbye.

You begin with questions such as "Can you tell me why you are so frustrated?" And you ask this as frequently as possible. First in one-on-one conversations. After a few rounds of much of the same, in public settings. In meetings. Whenever you can help the person to see that they are exhibiting a pattern of behavior that is both negative and repetitive.

And then you start some very direct conversations following the observation with these statements.

You seem unhappy here.

You seem very angry when seemingly trivial things occur.

How do you see this getting better?

How can I help you make it better?

After giving them time to think, ask the big question….**do you think it is time to move on?** If they bristle, if they are adamant they are going to stay, if they promise they are happy, despite appearing otherwise, continue to hold them to the fire. Continue to call them out when they exhibit negative behaviors. Continue to let them know you notice their unhappiness. And then one of two things will happen. They will either begin to do better or they will begin to look elsewhere. And while that goodbye is tougher than others, because they are producing good things, they are also making other things, those can't see them things but crucial to organizational success things, more difficult. Removing the controllable that is causing unrest in uncontrolled areas will serve you well in the long run, even if it at first appears to be a huge loss. And you are in this game for the long run, so always play to that end goal.

Virtual Spark Applications:

- Use data to show trends. Particularly historical data unique to this employee. Track negative comments in meetings and emails. Then present it when the time is right.
- Specifically ask the question "Are you here because it is a virtual space? Is the ease and comfort of your location the only reason you stay?"
- Keep track of participation in meetings/platforms/extras and point out the lack of interest in organizational culture and goals.

TOO MANY COOKS IN THE KITCHEN

I was at Walmart with my entire family doing the self-checkout thing. I know there are STRONG opinions about this option, but that is not the point of this chapter. The point is that we were all jumping in trying to get through the checkout process as quickly as possible. I was identified as the scanner, my husband was the bagger, my middle daughter was the one who would take the bags and put them in the cart, and my son was the one to oversee the whole process and jump in when things were getting backed up. The littlest was just to stay out of the way as much as a 6-year-old can.

Well, right from the word go it was a DISASTER. There is a reason the check-out line has one scanner and one bagger. Because our experience went something like this:

Me barking orders while attempting to find the barcodes as quickly as possible.

My husband yelling that I was throwing things down too quickly, thus causing everything to fall over.

My daughter yelling at my son for not reacting quickly.

My son yelling at my six-year-old for getting in the way.

A random employee showing up asking to see my ID for the bottle of wine (keeping in mind I am almost fifty years old with three children and one husband driving me to madness)

To say this was an exercise in inefficiency and wasted effort is an understatement.

Now, let's apply a similar scenario to the work setting….

I planned a retreat for our staff leaders. There were approximately fifty attending. I initially handled everything. Finding the hotel. Securing the location. Picking out the food. Choosing the meeting spaces. Etc. Etc. Etc. But as we got closer and closer to the event, several of my leadership team members became involved. My director of operations by attempting to help with some of the rooming lists. My right-hand woman by attempting to help with the meeting spaces and food options.

There were many emails between the three of us and the hotel itself. And things got messy quickly. I repeatedly said to the women both as a whole and individually, "Y'all, I got this. Let me have it." But, for some reason, they did not listen. I am not sure if they thought I COULDN'T handle it, or they just didn't want me to handle it. Either way, things got canceled that should not have been and then had to be added back, causing more work for all kinds of people. All coming from a place of supposed help and care. And this help and care literally continued right up until the moment of the retreat and probably only ended because there was no further need to plan because the planning part was over.

Why do we continuously group sabotage when we can clearly see the group approach is not working? I think it is for two reasons.

One, and this is where we get ourselves in trouble, it is because we got into leadership to lead. And so, we think we must lead everything.

And two, if we aren't leading, well, we fear things might go crazy or sideways.

What's a sparky leader to do? At the checkout line or at the catering line? The answer to both is to step away. Even if you were the first there, scanning those barcodes and picking those sandwich boxes. If someone repeatedly is stepping in and stepping on toes and the outcome is inconsequential, well then let them do it………. I know. Did you just shake a little??? Cause guess what? In both scenarios, I did not step away! In fact, I stepped closer and firmer and harder! I pushed people away repeatedly with

"I got this…. go back to bagging!"

"Go back to doing something else."

"I can handle it."

But by continuing to do the thing, and not allowing others to do the thing, you participate in this never-ending cycle that causes that overlap of inefficiency and confusion.

The second reason we all want to be in the kitchen is because we think our way is the best way. We may not really WANT to pick the sandwiches or bag the groceries BUT we think we do it just a teeny bit better than the next gal so, we gotta do it or it won't be 100 percent perfect. The catering choices will be good, but not great. The room will be set up ok, but not exceptionally. The bags will be packed nicely but not geometrically. If we do it, it will be A+ work; if someone else does it, it may just be A caliber.

And let's say all that is true, even though it really isn't. Is there anything wrong with A work? Or 99% instead of 100%? Or good over great? Especially when it allows someone in your organization to grow and flourish? When it allows your sous chef to become THE chef? Well, I would say then it becomes A+, exceptional, super-duper work.

Instead of pushing people out of the kitchen, even when it is YOUR kitchen, go ahead and take the step out. When you recognize the number in the kitchen is making it inefficient, don't push out others, just remove yourself and maybe another leader to allow those that don't often cook the opportunity. In the case of the Walmart scenario, I wish more than anything I would have allowed my son the chance to scan the groceries....... The kid is about to go off to college and lord knows he needs all the life skills he can get (probably because he has a mom who leads All. The. Time.) I wish I had let one of my assistant principals lead up the leadership retreat. Because I and the other two ladies fighting over the task do it All. The. Time. And someone else needs to learn to love to lead these ropes and navigate these waters.

Leading is so very much like cooking. We are all hoping to create that perfect meal and serve it up at the right moment. But to make that meal complete we need to ensure the right people are in the right place at the right time. We all know that it takes timing and delegation, but what we often forget or choose to ignore is that it often requires us to step away from the heat and move out into the main dining room and let others fire up the grill, plate up the entree, and clean up the dishes. We lay all the plans, direct all the chefs but then trust that they can carry out and execute them to make great things occur. When we allow those things to happen, truly great things will occur in our kitchens, even without our active participation!

Virtual Spark Applications:

- In the virtual space, you may find yourself with a multitude of volunteers/leaders/participants due to the ease of availability and flexible nature of the work. Set clear parameters before asking for staff to serve. Come up with an application process, a number needed, and a clear outline of responsibilities. This will help narrow the field and ensure you aren't trying to collaborate with 50 people on something that only required 5.

- Delegate. Delegate. Delegate. This is easier to do in the virtual setting than in a face-to-face collaboration. Assign tasks, send staff out to complete them on their own, and then come back together to share out.
- If there are too many virtual cooks, let some leave the kitchen! Ask for volunteers and then remember to seek them out the next time you need a sous chef or a pastry maker.

STUCK IN A RUT AND WORKING
TO GET OUT

LIFE IS, well, A. Lot.

And the older you get, the **more** it gets. Work. Family. Fun. Commitments. Health. Wealth. Home. The list is endless. You will feel pulled in all the directions and give pieces of yourself at each stop. Your exhaustion will be real. Your mental well-being will be spent. You will feel the need to do a lot of nothing even though you need to do almost everything.

How do you balance all this? The pull to the everything with the need to focus on you. The ability to STOP even though that seems counterintuitive. It is NOT easy, but it IS doable. Much like everything in life worth having, it requires vigilance and planning.

Here's real life, in this exact moment, an example of getting unstuck. It is literally happening right as I write these words.

I am stuck in the in between. Wanting nothing more than to finish writing this book and to use the words and the publication as a vehicle in which to spread my wings and fly out into the great unknown. To begin to share my message of the paramount importance of sparkly leadership and virtual shine to anyone in need. However, I am in a role with a high level of stress and a huge time commitment in a season of my life in which I need a considerable amount of less of both.

What am I to do?

Well, here is what I am doing. I am getting started. I am just doing it. I am writing this book amid various levels of roles and responsibilities. I am making getting unstuck a priority instead of a hope and a wish and a dream. I have begun.

Getting unstuck can be as simple as just that. Taking that first initial step. No matter how small. No matter how slow. Just doing something. Because you will take a step. And then another. And then another. Until you have moved into a space that allows you to finally separate and fully move on to the next big thing. Important to note is that sometimes those steps might have lots of time between them. It literally might be weeks or even months between one step and the next. And that is OK. Just doing it is key and will allow you the peace of mind to know you are moving towards something as opposed to remaining stagnant. And that, in and of itself, will be the biggest accomplishment to help that continued trajectory.

Let's start REAL SMALL. Like the tiniest incremental bit of change, for those of you that are change adverse. Or not doing it all adverse. Or guilt ridden when you do anything for you. Stop what you are doing right this very minute and get up your Google Calendar/day planner/scheduler and immediately create a weekly, 30-minute recurring event titled "just for me." Put it on a day and time when you know you will have the most freedom. AND give yourself permission to move (NOT delete) if something comes up that requires your attention during that block. And then, when that appointment time comes, do something for you.

Anything. Read a book. Take a walk. Make a snack. Watch a show. Listen to a podcast. Call your bestie. Whatever fills your cup, do it. Just promise it is not work related and not family related and not anyone else but you related. You deserve these 30 minutes, so take them!

Once you have mastered this task, consider extending it to an hour a week. Or two 30-minute blocks. Or heck, go crazy and do something for yourself daily. The rewards will be great.

Next up....... Prioritize your tasks.

What are your must dos? Your love to dos? Your don't need to do but you still dos? Your someone else should dos? Figure out what you do not need to do anymore and STOP or delegate. This frees up the ever-elusive time to allow you to focus on what only you can and should be doing AND gives you more time to do the things you most love.

Now, I get it.... letting go can be haaaaaarrrrrrrrrrrd-dddddddddd. And scary. Because what if your spouse loads the dishwasher "incorrectly"? Or that person leading the meeting doesn't say it just like you would say it? OR, and this is the scariest thought of all, what if all the things you love are not what you should be doing and you hate all the rest? (We will revisit this idea below).

However, I promise you, and this is a big promise which might seem inflated or just words from someone who has no clue about you. But I promise you.... It. Will. Be. Ok.

Because you are not delegating the big things. You are just letting go. And once you do that, and embrace that, you will realize some of what you were holding on to was fluff. Was forced. Was unnecessary. Was being done by you because it has always been done by you and no one else thought they could or should do it.

And here is the beauty in the letting go. You can always take it back. There are times you may have to take back. Your job or your home will require it. But only take back temporarily. Fix why this task is coming back your way and then send it right on back new and improved.

Finally, craft a new you.

You focused on finding your Zen each week and you got rid of some things......this SHOULD have freed you up to focus on the next steps in your personal journey. Now that you have the time and the mental resolve, where do YOU go next? Can you take on something exciting and new? Can you revamp something that needed fixing? Where are you going and how will you get there? Once again, be intentional with your time. Add blocks to brainstorm new systems and ways. Find time to research new processes and procedures. Get with the people that can help put your new plans in motion.

However, if you realized that you have given away everything you love and the rest is just, meh, if nothing new and exciting and innovative for your role is an option or even something you desire, then I would say this.......... your time where you are may have come to an end. I know. SUPER SCARY! I get it! However, there is nothing more detrimental to an organization than a sparkless leader. Someone who is just there because they have been there forever. Someone tired, burnt out, and bored. Goodness, if that someone is you, take the steps immediately to find the place that will excite and energize you. And the beauty of being proactive is that YOU control the journey. You write the narrative. You set the pace. And what you may find in your quest for new, is that in the interim you start to fix what is broken where you are, which may, in turn lead you back.... crazy how that can happen!

Spark for life is the key to everything. Without it, you are just there. Take the time to seek it out and utilize it for your greater good. All that you touch will be better for it.

Virtual Spark Applications:

- Find a tool to track your joy. This "tool" can be as simple as a notebook in which you journal or a Google Doc in which you take notes throughout your day. And then measure your emotions for a period. Rank the tasks you are completing daily and review to see if you are experiencing more bleh than yay!
- SET BOUNDARIES! The virtual world allows for a constant influx of noise. Emails never stop dinging. Texts never stop pinging. Virtual meetings and tasks are super easy to schedule. Turn off the notifications from time to time. Hold firm to the calendar you set and do not move things. Put you first every single day!
- Make a pros and cons list. And add to it daily. Review after a set period to determine if there are a copious amount of more on either side and use that to determine how quickly you need to get unstuck.

WHEN LEAVING BREAKS YOUR HEART

YOU EVER BEEN the last person to leave a party? Or a bar? Or an amusement park? Or sporting event? Did you stay 'til the very last minute, even though you knew it was over, just to continue to savor the moment and relish in the memories for a teeny bit more time? Knowing that the lights are about to come on, the clean-up is about to start, and tomorrow will be bittersweet? You know it is time to go; it is over, and yet you want to hang on just as long as possible.

That is exactly where I am as I write these words. I have been at my organization for over fourteen years. I have helped to grow it from a small, unknown entity to one that is an exemplar for best practice. I have served in a variety of leadership roles, with the most recent being the one all the way at the top. I have loved the build. I have loved the growth. I have loved the revolutionary outside of the box thinking that was required along the way. But above all else I have loved the relationships I have made and experiences we have shared.

But as I sit here reflecting on the last fourteen years, I realize, I am one of the last at the party. Those that came in with me have long since left. New faces, which I love just as much as the old, began to tend to all the things, leaving me with nostalgia and sometimes loneliness. I have put in a lot of blood, sweat, and tears to make this place a little better, a little brighter than it was when I arrived. And now I know my work is done. I have known for a while now. And I know that closing time is here.

But oh, is it hard to say goodbye. Even when you know it is time. Especially after fourteen years. Especially after great success. Especially after lots of love and fun and connections. Heck, everything in this book I learned during my time at this wonderful place. So, yes, I am sitting here, hoping for one last encore, one last drink, one last dance.

I know the lights are about to come on at my party. It is last call. Time to head on home. I know that in my bones. I have done great work here and now it is time to allow others to step into the spotlight.

I also know the next party will be super bright. That there is so much for me to do there and give there and share there. I am THRILLED to start that party! I am just hating the thought of leaving what I have loved. But I know, due to the culture and community we worked to create the party I am leaving will continue to also be super bright. Because that, my friends, is the best part of being a sparky leader. It is instilling a little bit of spark, a little bit of chaos, a little bit of big celebration, a little bit of fire and confetti and shine in those that you support and knowing they will carry that light within them for the rest of their days. When you see that light coming from those in which you have led, you will know it is closing time and you will feel confident in your decision to leave, as you are certain that the spark will never die out. It will be your lasting legacy.

HOPE

ABOUT TEN YEARS after our school opened, we were identified by the state of South Carolina as needing improvement. A Transformation Coach was assigned and showed up at our back-to-school meeting. She was nice enough. Sort of Mary Poppins prim and proper, minus the medicine bag and umbrella. Friendly, but businesslike. Kind, yet ready to get to work. She sat at a table in the back, smiling at all the appropriate moments, talking when spoken to, but writing, writing, writing. I don't think she stopped writing the entire time she was there. Not sure what she was writing. But PHEW! Was that intimidating! And at the end of the meeting, she very nicely and politely thanked me for the lovely meeting, let me know she was leaving to give me time with my staff and would be in touch with me within the next week. To say I wasn't sad to see her go was an understatement.

Upon her departure, my staff gave a collective sigh of relief. Some of the comments were:

"Was she a spy?"

"Was she trying to catch us doing something wrong?"

"How long is she going to be with us?"

and one of my favorites, from one of my favorite staff members ever (and let's not pretend we don't all have favorites, because we do)

"Alicia, I think the state department should spend more time fixing themselves than fixing us cause we are doing pretty awesome, comparatively speaking."

I can't say I disagreed with them, at first. I can't say I wasn't exceptionally annoyed at the fact that we were making tremendous gains and would continue to do so, if just given a bit more time, and didn't need a "babysitter". I can't say I didn't think the presence of this woman was, in fact, a waste of taxpayer dollars and that there weren't other schools that were more in need of support. However, I am also someone who knows that you don't turn help away when you aren't perfect. If we had already reached our goals, if we had been perfect already, then sure, we could say, we don't need you. But we weren't there yet, so we couldn't say, "Thanks but no thanks,".

The next week, the Transformation Coach and I met virtually, and I instantly realized this lady was pretty darn amazing and OMG wickedly smart. Like so brilliant you need a dictionary and a thesaurus to fully understand the words she uses. But not so smart that she makes you feel dumb. Just so intelligent you know you are in the presence of greatness. She was funny. Soooooooooooooooo funny. In a dry, witty, way. She was also oh so kind. And caring. And supportive. Like, she REALLY wanted to help. And she REALLY wanted us to succeed. And not just cause the state department said you need to succeed or we will shut you down. But because she was in our corner cheering all the way.

She was not at all aggressive. Not pushy. Even though her job was all about impacting change. And I am certain her boss at the state department was constantly asking her to demonstrate growth and data showing improvements, but she never put the pressure on us. She just trusted that the measures we were taking to make changes were going to result in goals being reached and thus improvements being made.

She was also **my** biggest cheerleader. In everything. She made me feel like a superstar. And a magic maker. And a difference maker. Like I could move mountains and drive change and literally do anything I set my mind to. And because she believed, I believed. And because I believed, my staff believed. And when the staff believed, the students believed……….and guess what happened??? We met our goals. Drove the change. Got off the state list. Said goodbye to our Transformation Coach.

Except I didn't. Because the Mary Poppins prim and proper lady sitting in the back of the staff meeting furiously taking notes quickly became my friend. My sounding board. My advisor. My confidant. My talking off the ledge supporter. When the Choose Your Own Adventure chapter happened to me, she was one of the first people I called. When leaving broke my heart, I reached out to her to reassure me that the leaving might break my heart, but the next chapter would be even better. And guess what? She is the entire reason I am even writing this book, as she is the one who said from the very start, "What you got here is pretty unique and special. The world needs to know about it!".

She gave me hope. Over and over and over. When the school was under the watchful eye of the state. When I was doubting the magic we were making. When I was wondering what was next. She was there. Inspiring. Cultivating. Making me bold. Making me brave. Making me move forward. In her calm and reassuring way. For that, I am forever grateful.

Here's the lesson for all y'all. Do not turn away help. Ever. Even if it is forced help. Even when it comes from the Evil

Empire. Even when it appears to be a Mary Poppins, prim and proper spy. It would have been easy to do. In fact, she has told me, many of her schools often have. They give her the cold shoulder and cursory breadcrumbs of items in which to help with. Cutting off their noses to spite their face. And I get it. On some levels, I do. Our pride gets in our way. But putting that aside is crucial because the payoff is bountiful.

For all of you ready to write the final chapter of your current book and to start the intro on the next one, I am here to tell you I know that is daunting. I am just hopeful that you have a Hope in your corner. I hope that you don't turn her or someone like her away. I am hopeful that your Hope is as fabulous as mine. She has been the difference maker in all that I have done and all that is to come. If you don't already have a Hope, get yourself one, forced or otherwise, and lean on in and rely on them in everything…for advice and guidance and idea bouncing and laughs and tears and partnerships and friendship and then write that last chapter and start the next book. Scary as it is, it is also bound to be filled with sunshine and rainbows and sparks and fireworks!

ACKNOWLEDGEMENTS

Where to begin? Because I would not have been able to do this if I hadn't a HUGE team of cheerleaders and supporters from the very start. So, I'll start there.......

To my parents, **Bonnie and Tony Picaro,** for instilling in me a love of reading from as far back as I can remember. Books were everything to me and let me travel the world. I didn't realize then, but writing became a love and a passion of mine and has allowed me great success in my career. So, thank you for the 100s of hours spent reading books like Spot and the Little Engine that Could and The Little House.

To alllllll the educators who have inspired me with their greatness and poured into me with their passion and commitment. From Mrs. **Ellen Plumly** at Southern Regional High School, who taught me relationships are so much more important than math, to **Professor Kennedy** at Winthrop University, who showed me teaching history can be excited and also allow for present day connections with students, to **Anita Huggins**, current Charleston County School District Superintendent, who gave the keynote speech on my first day as a teacher, and made me think "hmmmmm maybe I can do more with this teaching degree than just teach!" And there are literally hundreds more I could name, as I have been so blessed to be taught by and work with the best of the best of the best.

To the amazing staff I had the pleasure of leading for so many years at South Carolina Connections Academy. Much like the paragraph above, there are just too many of you to name! But I am certain you recognize your stories in these pages. **Joseph C**, my eccentric bestie who taught me about Lion's Gates, **Sam G**, who was always "Team Alicia" even when it wasn't cool, **Tracey W**, who could make me laugh, even in the worst of times, **Catayah C**, for being a quiet, yet complete and total rock star in all you did, **Shea H**, who took inspiration in my thriving in chaos and helped reign me in from time to time, **Jenny D**, for your patience and attention to alllllll the details, and, well, after 14 years, and over 1000 employees during those years, I literally COULD write a whole 'nother book and fill it with stories of admiration for each of you..........so THANK YOU. Thank you for allowing me to grow with you as we navigated the brave new world of virtual education.

To the Educated Dragons. **Patrick and Hope Dugan.** This literally would not have happened without each of you. So, thank you for always believing in me, even when I was doubtful. And for helping me get this book to print. Would not have taken any of these steps without you pushing me along.

To my Tribe. My Chosen Family. My Besties. **Jenny, Dubbs, Erin, Rob, Matt, Todd.** You all will never know how much your presence in my life has gotten me through it all. From the challenges of parenthood. To the challenges of adulting. To the challenges of aging. To the challenges of work. You all have been there through every single good time and every single tough time. With laughter. And tissues. And hugs. And Red Label Buds. And saltwater therapy. And concerts. And late Saturday nights. And early morning school drop offs. Could not get through this thing called life without you all.

To my children. **Rentz, Haven, and Poppy.** You three are the reason for every single thing I do. I want you to know the power of positivity and the importance of relationships. I want you to understand that being true to you is about the only thing that matters, beyond being kind to others. And I want you to remember that you can do anything you set your mind to. This book is proof of that!

And finally, to my husband. **Rusty Hughes.** I literally could not do any of this without your undying support and loyalty. And I mean ANY of it. Not just the writing of the book. The launching of the business, while being a mom, and keeping up with all the things that need to be done, all while enjoying all the things that make life worth living. You are my biggest supporter, my constant companion, my ride or die (usually on a boat), my concert singing partner, my #HOLO loving adventurer who keeps me laughing and grounded and motivated and inspired. Just like Cinderella got her Prince Charming and lived happily every after, so did I. Forever grateful for you and our life and so looking forward to 50 more years of living the dream with you!

www.ingramcontent.com/pod-product-compliance
Lightning Source LLC
Chambersburg PA
CBHW051526120626
46551CB00012B/1090